DARK PSYCHOLOGY AND MANIPULATION MIND

Stop Having Y(

271 Pages Of Strategies And

Tricks Allowing The Most Powerful And

Influential Men On Earth To Influence And

Dominate The Mind Of Anyone, Also Yours

DONALD BELFORT

Chapter 1. Introduction

At its root, dark psychology is all about mind control. You can influence what other people think or do by understanding the inner workings of the other person's mind. You can motivate people to help you by helping them first. You know that they are more likely to offer help if you allow them first simply because people tend to reciprocate. When you understand how the minds of those around you work, you can begin utilizing it to your advantage.

Dark psychology is used widely throughout a wide range of scenarios, some of which are more sinister, while others are typically seen as far less harmful. Each of the following groups utilizes dark psychology concepts to get the desired results: religion, politics, cults, terrorist organizations, abusers, and salespeople. They all rely heavily on dark psychology concepts, pulling strings behind other people's backs to get what they want.

Religion

Religion is all about conformity. You are required to conform to a specific set of beliefs, into which you are most frequently indoctrinated as children and then encouraged to follow through adulthood. Though it may seem harmless, religion uses several dark psychology techniques to keep people in line and follow the doctrine. Typically, this is seen as some sort of threat or punishment if you do not follow through — it could be going to hell instead of some kind of paradise or heaven after death, or it could be a threat of excommunication and abandonment. These threats play upon two huge fears of people — losing community and a threat of eternal suffering, and people are more likely to obey.

Politics

Political leaders often engage in several different dark psychology techniques useful in manipulating other people's minds. They hold themselves in specific ways, describe things that make the people believe they can better empathize, and speak in ways that inspire other people to follow them. They often use slippery slope fear-mongering tactics, promising results that no one will like if peopleoppose them. They use stances meant to convey power and authority, and people fall for it. People fall for the artificial body language that the politicians use, and the politicians win out.

Cults

Cults, especially destructive cults, are incredibly exploitative. They are considered totalistic — meaning they seek to gain control over the other person entirely. They frequently engage in various forms of thought reform to gain control over the other person's mind. These cults rely on authoritarian following and leading to a wide range of manipulative tactics. Cults rely on their leaders' charisma, deception, isolation, methods of thought-reform, demands for loyalty and devotion, creating a divide between those who follow the cult and outsiders, cult language or jargon that is difficult to understand and follow if you are not a member and as much control as possible over the day-to-day existence of the members. All of this culminates in a group that seeks to manipulate and control the members in a way that demands absolute loyalty. This is how people get sucked in — they are drawn in with false promises, and their

personality and thoughts are whittled away, bit by bit, day by day, until finally, all that is left behind is a tool for the cult to use. When under the cult's leaders' control, the leader can command nearly anything, and the followers will do so. This makes them so destructive that the members are essentially turned into mindless weapons, willing to do whatever it takes to stay in favor.

Terrorism

Terrorism groups follow similar cults to get people in line — promising the world for their absolute devotion. They draw people in with idealized values and charismatic leaders and whittle the people away until they are willing to do anything, even if it involves suicide. They see themselves as a part of the whole, a part of the change that they will use to change the world for the better, and they are glad to give their very lives, or the lives of their loved ones, to achieve it.

Abuse

Abusers love to utilize dark psychology — they use the minds' inner workings to weasel their ways into their victims' lives. They firmly root themselves as integral members while taking advantage of people's tendency to keep their

relationships meaningful. The abuser's love bombs the victim, meaning he showers the victim in love, attention, and affection to hook the victim to him before suddenly revoking the attention, making the victim crave it and do anything necessary to get the love back. This sort of manipulation tactic and use of dark psychology is often seen with narcissists, in particular, to understand what the narcissist wants.

Sales Even something as innocent as sales can be littered with dark psychology tactics. The best salespeople can intuitively convince people to buy, tapping into unconscious tendencies, appeals to emotions, and even hijacking the other person's body language to achieve the desired result. Salespeople get paid based on their sales, so they will do anything necessary to get the desired results. They will appeal to a parent's fear of a car accident to upsell to a safer vehicle and use a person's near-death experience as a segue into selling life insurance. They will change their body language to convince the other person, picking up on small cues here and there and acting upon them to get the desired results.

So, let's understand something more about dark psychology.

Chapter 2. What is Emotional Intelligence?

Emotional Intelligence is the ability to be aware, understand, and control personal emotions. A person with emotional intelligence can also understand others' emotions and feel them as if they were going through such emotions. Emotional intelligence involves some skills, which are:

Emotional awareness: this is   the skill that helps you realize your emotions regarding what you feel. Most people are not aware of their feelings and for this, they cannot tell when they are happy, sad, angry or depressed. If you need to work on yourself, you need to be aware of what exactly you are going through. You can also explain to others exactly what they put you through, something most people struggle with. When you can describe your emotions, others will know how to handle you or even know how to help you overcome the feelings. Emotional intelligence goes beyond personal awareness because just as you can label your emotions, you can also label others' emotions around you. You will be aware when they are happy or need your help because you can tell their feelings.

Understanding

- once you are aware of your emotions, it is easier to understand them in terms of what causes them, and how often they recur.

This means that when dealing with others, you will understand what will cause them pain or what will restore their joy. This means that as a person with high EQ, you are empathetic towards others and once in a while, you will have to put yourself in their shoes. By doing this, you will now view things in their eyes and understand them better as individuals without being too judgmental.

Control

- when you are aware and understand the emotions you and the people in your life go through, you can control them. You avoid situations that provoke the anger in you and avoid people who bring out the worst. When dealing with others, you can also avoid doing or saying things that will cause them. You can regulate the emotions you go through and those of others, but you can look for solutions. You are now in a position where you can help yourself and others become better than the emotions coming your way. Usually, this entails anger management, knowing how to deal when anger strikes you or the people around you. This means that you will need to be flexible once and adapt to people with different ideologies from yours and be open-minded. It also means that you have to take responsibility when necessary and also be trustworthy and practice integrity.

Social skills

- a person who has a high EI can communicate better with others. They are better listeners as well, and people find it easier to confide in them. Communication skills are also paramount in the workplace since you will negotiate and maintain clients. This skill also makes people with high EI become better problem solvers and can solve conflicts amongst themselves or between other people.

Most emotional intelligence critics argue that it does not exist simply because it cannot be measured like the Intelligent Quotient. They, therefore, say that emotional intelligence is just an interpersonal skill that is being labeled differently. However, emotional intelligence continues to be very popular and proves that, indeed, being emotionally intelligent is much needed in every human being who wants to succeed all around.

According to the World economic forum, emotional intelligence is the number six out of the ten skills people need to work in their workplace. It is for this reason that most employers have introduced dynamic intelligence tests as part of job interviews. This is because people with high intelligence are the best team leaders that any organization can hire. An emotionally intelligent employee also performs better than any other employee and that is why it is crucial to find employees who have some level of emotional intelligence. Emotion intelligence also consists of social skills that help you deal with your family, friends, workmates, and relationships. Some people can make friendships quickly but cannot maintain the networks because they lack social skills from emotional intelligence. People with high emotional intelligence can relate better with their friends and their relationships work better since they understand the people in their lives. When a person with high emotional intelligence is dealing with people, they can identify things that will frustrate them and keep away from them. On the other hand, people with high emotional intelligence can tell when someone is being overly sensitive and will be able to stay away from them until they are calm and reasonable.

You must know having a high EI doesn't make you different from others. You will still be predisposed to both negative and positive emotions. Anyone who wants to achieve emotional intelligence must work hard to ensure that they are only entertaining positive thoughts. Whenever negative thoughts strive, one should be able to reframe to positive thoughts. To achieve this, you have to ensure that you are always trying to be a better person each day. It's not going to be easy, but everyone can be emotionally intelligent since it is a skill that can be learned.

Characteristics of Emotional Intelligence

A Great overall balance- being able to strike a balance of all the activities you need to do every day can be overwhelming. Sometimes because of how much is expected of a person, people easily become stressed. An emotionally intelligent person can overcome that by finding a balance that will allow them to find peace and happiness despite the challenging circumstances. When such a person realizes that work, relationships are getting them worked up. They know how to step back, take a break, and find themselves first.

On the other hand, when there is a lack of emotional intelligence, people will get worked up by every little thing because they do not play and the time to work. Such people will continue doing the same thing repeatedly instead of finding something different or a different strategy. This is because they are not aware of how much affects their emotions and will always be angry and frustrated. Therefore, if you find someone who can still strike a balance in everything and is always happy even when everything is not working out, someone with a high EI.

Great Focus: Ever seen people who are easily distracted at anything they do? One minute they are so focused, and then after a small distraction, they are no longer as focused? That is someone who is controlled by their emotions. Such people will only work depending on their current moods. If they are angry at someone in their workplace who is in their team, they will refuse to work with that person simply because they are angry. This will then affect their performance because they have allowed their emotions to control them.

On the other hand, people with high EI are always focused no matter how overwhelming their work is. Sometimes there is so much to do that it may lead to confusion as you do not know what to do or where to start and that can bring worry which will cause distractions. The difference between those who lack high EI and those who have it is that those who do have laser focus.

Easy going: Sometimes, people think that having a high means that you always get everything right. However, this is not necessarily true because every human being faces different challenges. Therefore, it is most likely that they will go through hard times, but they are easy and understand that it is part of life. People who do not have EI tend to be very shaken by tough times and never move past that. They will always focus on their failures and forget all the success they have achieved over time. If they do not get something right, they think that they have now become life failures. These kinds of people usually try to do things correctly and if it didn't work out, they become frustrated. The people with EI

know that no one is perfect, and therefore, they understand that there will be downs and ups and, therefore, embrace this so well. Any mistake they make they can brush that off and move on from it.

Open-minded: Remember one of the skills a person with EI has a great understanding of others' emotions. This means that they can understand other people's perspectives. They are therefore very open-minded and will always consider the opinion of people around them. On the other hand, people who lack EI are very stubborn and only want to be heard. They feel like they are always right and always want their idea or opinion to be the only discussion subject. You are very likely to end up in a very bad argument with such people as you try to reason with them on a different perspective from theirs. They will also be easily offended because they do not expect you to argue with them when trying to express themselves.

Guarded: EI doesn't mean that someone will always be able to control their emotions. They are only able to control or regulate to a certain extent. However, sometimes it can be too much to handle. What people with EI do is predict how certain people and situations will negatively affect them. They will, therefore, avoid such people and conditions

because they understand that happiness is in their own hands.

On the other hand, people who lack EI think that people will make them happy and find it hard to stand for themselves. While a person with a high EI will say no when the situations don't favor them, people who like it will struggle to do that and, therefore, get angry and frustrated. This is because they were not able to stop the misfortunes in time; instead, they just rely on the current mood which may, in the long run, bring them a bad outcome. If you want to be like a high EI person, you have always to consider the current moods and whatever mood you are likely to have after some hours. This is because something exciting you now may in the afterward moment bring you regrets. On the other hand, you may find that something or someone who you have not connected with at the moment may turn out to be very rewarding in the end.

Chapter 3. Why do we need emotions?

In many years, psychologists and philosophers have been having a spirited debate on emotions and their various types like happiness and sadness. They have been trying to determine their nature if perceptions about different philosophical dynamics or cognitive judgments are about the satisfaction of set objectives. Different neuroscience theories explain several suggestions on how a human being's brain can generate emotions by combining bodily perceptions and cognitive appraisals. Suppose something thrilling in your life happens to you today. In that case, it is natural and very normal to develop an array of emotions such as happiness or sadness if it is a paining situation. There is a dualist view, traditional, that explains that a human being's body consists of a soul and a body. In this case, the soul is believed to be the one that experiences all mental states and emotions. However, this view can be disregarded and just termed as a motivated inference or a wishful thought since there is no substantial evidence that immortality and the soul exist.

Today, there are two main approaches, scientific approaches, that can be employed to explain what emotions are and their nature. Cognitive appraisal theory is one of the methods and it explains that emotions can be said to be judgments on how the situation you are in currently meets the goals you have set. According to this theory, emotions such as happiness are believed to be an expression of fulfilled dreams. On the other hand, sadness and emotions depict unfulfilled dreams and disappointments in life and can refer to a form of anger towards a stumbling block to your goals. Another theory that tries to explain what emotions are is that of William James together with others. They came up with an argument that emotions are just perceptions of various changes in your body in different situations. These body changes that depict emotions include mental reactions and physiological stages in life.

These two theories, psychological perception, and cognitive appraisal can be integrated to develop a unified definition of emotions. Understanding these theories makes it crystal clear that the mind controls and determines all sensations and perceptions based on the different situations. Therefore, we can describe emotions as one's mental state associated

with their nervous system linked to the body's chemical changes. These chemical changes are usually linked to your feelings, thoughts, degree of displeasure, pleasure, and behavioral responses. Emotions can also be termed as negative or positive experiences related to specific patterns of physiological functions in the body. The bottom line is that emotions are responsible for all the cognitive, behavioral, and physiological changes that we undergo in our bodies and how we react to them.

Basic Emotional Responses There are various types of emotions with different natures and varying influence in how we conduct ourselves when with other people and even generally how we live. These emotions if not controlled they may tend to control us. They can even harm the choices that we make in life. Apart from that, these emotions are a determiner to our thoughts in different situations that we face daily. Understanding these emotional responses will also give us a strong foundation to discuss how we can use them to rewire our bodies and minds to attain a better and healthier life.

Happiness This is one of the emotions that people have used different approaches to attain it thus tends to be vital. Happiness is a nice emotional state that depicts feelings of joy, contentment, well-being, gratification, and satisfaction. This emotional state is usually expressed through facial expressions like smiling, body languages like a relaxed stance and even a pleasing voice tone.

Sadness This is another emotional state that is the opposite of happiness and is depicted by feelings such as grief, hopelessness, dampened mood, disinterest, and disappointment. This is a widespread emotional state due to different stressful life experiences that we undergo daily. Having prolonged sadness might be hazardous to your health, specifically mental health since it can advance over time to become fatal depression. Its severity usually varies as it depends on the cause and the extent at which you can cope up with it.

Fear Fear is a mighty emotional state that plays a vital role in one's survival. When faced by danger or any situation that seems threatening, you will get into a flight or fight response situation. At this point, you will find that your muscles become tensed and with an increased heartbeat and respiration rate. This will trigger you to either fight the danger or run away from it instead. This emotion is usually depicted by widening eyes and other psychological reactions like rapid breathing and heartbeat.

Disgust Disgust is an emotional state that happens when you are disappointed or bored due to failure to achieve something. It can also be as a result of unpleasant sight, smell, or taste. This emotion can be depicted by the tendency to move away from disgusting you, other reactions like retching or vomiting and even facial expressions like curling your upper lip. This emotion might even make you to hate forever something that once disgusted you which can be hazardous.

Anger   Anger is one of the most significant and potent emotions depicted by agitation, hostility, antagonism, and frustration. Just as fear, it is also capable of triggering your flight or fight response. There are various ways in which anger is usually displayed and they include facial expressions like frowning. Body languages like turning down someone in a harsh manner can also be a sign of anger.

Identifying Emotions To use your emotions the right way, you need first to identify the emotions the right way. Let us look at the best way to determine the feelings:

Understand the Trigger

The first step towards identifying the emotion is first to know what caused it. This will help you to describe the events that led to the emotional event. In this step, try to stick to facts alone.

You can write down the event that led to the emotion to have it clear in your mind.

Why Do You Think It Happened? The following step is to identify the possible causes that led to the emotional event. This is crucial because it determines the meaning that you give to the situation that happened. The type of emotional event that led to the issue will determine how you react to the event in question.

How the Situation Made You Feel?   The following step is to determine how the emotional event made you feel both physically and emotionally. This will help you see whether the emotion resulted in a positive or negative reaction.

You need to notice both the positive and negative emotional and physical reactions you felt when it happened. Notice any physical feelings that you experience, such as tightness in the body.

What Was Your Reaction   You need to ask yourself this question so that you understand your urges. However, for the process to be effective, you need to make sure you are sincere. It might be painful to admit some of the urges that you felt when the event happened. When we face some situations, we at times

get strange urges to react differently. Some of the emotions that we go through might make us regret on the future.

You need to compare your reaction at the moment that things happened and how you usually react. This will tell you whether you managed to control the urge, or you failed to do so.

What Did You Do and Say?   The following step would be to understand what you said or did due to the emotions. Even though you didn't manage to respond correctly, you need to be honest with yourself about how you handled the situation. You also need to understand how the decision you made impacted on the situation. This can be a good learning experience for you.

Once you evaluate your reaction, you can then use the situation to learn how to handle another condition that might arise.

5 Common Emotions Experienced by Humans

Jealousy   Jealousy is a combination of different emotional reactions against the success of another person. The responses include; anger, fear, and anxiety about not being the privilege's primary owner. Research has it that both women and men tend to be jealous because of various reasons. For example, when a woman believes her rival is more beautiful than her, it is likely to spark some jealousy. However, it is normal for practically everyone to experience some level of resentment. When caring about someone or something important, you may become anxious with the thought of losing the person or that something to somebody else.

What is Depression?   Being depressed involves your body, moods, and thoughts you will be having from time to time. When one is affected by depression, the way they deal with life becomes different. The way you eat, how you feel, and interact with people becomes different. Depression is a disorder, and it is tough to deal with it all by yourself.

If you notice you have depression or someone is affected by it, advise them to seek medical help. When you get the right support, everything will be fine. Being depressed means, you will experience feelings of sadness that will last for an extended period. You will eventually lose interest in things that shape your life. Remember that people who are depressed do not acknowledge who they are. When one depressed, it does not mean you have a weakness or are experiencing inadequacy. It is an illness that requires professional medical help.

What is Anger? Renown investigators like Berkowitz, who spend most of their time dealing with psychology, defines anger as a strong feeling of annoyance, displeasure, or hostility. It is also considered a normal, healthy feeling that allows one to convey a reaction to a given situation. As much as it is reasonable to feel angry, the same attitude can be harmful if you express it in a way that upset you or the people around you. Everyone has had a feeling of anger, and everybody has a way of dealing with the sentiment.

The bible has covered the topic of anger comprehensively. The verses that talk about anger are numerous, but we will only mention a few. We should avoid responding to people with a negative attitude since it stimulates anger. Another famous verse about anger is proverbs 22:24 that strongly condemn us not to befriend hot-tempered people.

What is Fear Fear is a natural feeling that everyone experiences frequently. It is something that you cannot avoid because it is a way of responding to severe sensations. It is easy to confuse fear with worry, anxiety, doubt, panic, and apprehension. The feeling of being afraid is the worst feeling that anybody would want to feel. It is uncomfortable, unpleasant, distressing, and at that point, you consistently try to come out of that situation. Everyone experiences fear in different ways; everyone is afraid of other things. This makes it challenging to come up with the right definition of fear.

Stress and Worry Stress is a natural human response when faced with challenging situations. Same as fear, the fight or flight action is triggered by the mind when stress is experienced. Stress might be positive or negative. It is positive when one's objectives are to be met; hence, more adrenaline is produced. For negative pressure, depression is always experienced, and one might go to killing himself or herself.

Chapter 4. How to manage emotional intelligence

Emotional intelligence is quite different from average intelligence. It is measured differently, too. Its scoring is used in several organizations since most employers have realized that people with high EQ perform better on the job than those with high IQ. This is because emotionally intelligent employees can remain calm during challenging circumstances. They are also able to resolve conflicts easily and lead others by example. Such employees are capable of making sound decisions on behalf of the organization, steering it forward.

EQ is, therefore, a valuable asset for managers, business owners, and human resources practitioners. Research shows that people with high EQ perform better than people with weak EQ. This is why emotional intelligence is considered a critical competency for all leadership positions. It can be applied to various organizations and life in general. Some of the applications of EQ include the following.

Coaching- EQ is used in training managers on how to relate with their team members. Emotional intelligence coaching helps people build better relationships, improve communication and decision-making, increase their engagement, and reduce stress levels.

Job success profiles—Emotional intelligence has been used successfully in the past to create job profiles. Most companies use these during recruitment since they contain behavioral skills that are essential for each profile.

Capability development – Most of the high performing leaders are more intelligent than their colleagues. Emotional intelligence helps leaders to improve their performance by maximizing their potential.

Training – EQ can be used to develop employee skills to enable them to perform on the job. Specialists use this to provide individual feedback on a wide array of platforms.

Team Building – emotional intelligence has a significant impact on team members and how they relate to each other. It increases the effectiveness of teams and helps improve interpersonal relationship skills. Some of the positive effects of emotional intelligence include:

• Improved learning. Emotional intelligence is a concept that can be easily understood. It is not hereditary and can be easily acquired. When studied adequately, it can improve a person's personality

- Eliminates destructive behavior. Empathy is one of the characteristics of emotional intelligence. In most cases, high emotional intelligence translates to good behavior.

- Better social interactions. Individuals with good emotional intelligence can relate well with others.

Emotional Intelligence and Career Success

Until recently, employers believed that technical skills were all that candidates required to excel in job positions. However, the concept of emotional intelligence has continuously proved that this is not true. People skills are as necessary as technical skills when it comes to business success. Nowadays, organizations are seeking individuals who are talented and can relate well with colleagues and customers.

When you understand your emotions and learn how to control them, you will quickly get along with others in the

workplace. EQ professionals link it to increased job satisfaction and higher salaries. While most people put a lot of emphasis on IQ, its importance can never be effective without incorporating it with EQ. One of the leading researchers on EQ, Daniel Goleman, once concluded that emotional intelligence is just as important as IQ as far as job success is concerned. Individuals who focus on developing their EQ on the job always grow faster in their careers than those who do not. If you ever dream of becoming a successful leader, you must invest in building your emotional intelligence.

The ability to understand your emotions and those of others, can come naturally in some people. More businesses and organizations are now focusing on developing this skill in their employees using online assessment tools. A wide array of practitioners offers these.

Emotional intelligence comprises of four primary skills. These are: 1. Self-awareness-self-awareness refers to the ability to understand our emotions and how they affect our reaction to circumstances and situations around us

2. Self-management. This is the ability to control our emotions and direct our characters in a positive and constructive manner

3. Social awareness, which means the ability to connect with other people's emotions and being mindful of their thoughts and feelings

4. Relationship management. This refers to the ability to use the three skills above to manage the day to day interactions

Every individual has a varying degree of emotional intelligence. However, this can be increased through various actions and training. As a career person and leader, there are several steps that you can take to ensure that emotional intelligence puts you ahead of other

• Start by understanding your emotion. For example, if you have a negative behavior such as resentment and anger, you can start practicing how to suppress this behavior

• After understanding yourself, concentrate on understanding how the people that surround you think and feel. In most office environments, people fear to share their emotions with their colleagues.

Understanding the emotions of others and allowing them to express themselves are some of the ways of building lasting relationships.re

• Lastly, establish some relationship-building strategies. Know when to work alone and when to collaborate with other employees.

Following these steps is critical for your professional success. EQ has the power and capability to steer you into senior roles within the organization. Most employees who earn good salaries attribute this to a high EQ. This is because they understand when to ask for a salary increment. They do not do this anyhow but wait for the perfect moment, and mode of asking appropriate for their supervisors. Such people also get pay rises quickly because they are always more productive than employees with low EQ. They also boast of good reputation because of their sharp relationship building skills.

Research shows that only 15% of career success can be attributed to technical skills. The other 85% is due to personality, human relations, and the ability to lead, communicate, and negotiate. This is how crucial emotional intelligence is. Most effective leaders use their high EQ to

build partnerships capable of helping them rise in their careers. High EQ also puts businesspersons on the competitive edge. Most customers will purchase a product from a salesperson that can engage them on a personal level. This explains why some not-so-good products sell better than great products.

Emotional Intelligence and Personal Relations Human beings are emotional creatures. Sometimes they can become hostile. Once in a while, you may encounter some individuals who do not value you or clients who treat you with contempt. How you react to such people will determine if your relationship with them will improve or deteriorate.

Some people always feel neglected and left out even when this is not the case. Such people suffer in silence for fear of speaking out. Emotional intelligence helps you to identify such people and motivate them into becoming a better version of themselves. It is critical to solve any emotional related issues in today's world since people deal with challenging situations every day. It is advisable to help others

find a solution to their problems since social awareness is one of the major components of emotional intelligence.

The goal of every leader is to cause impact. When put together, individual achievements translate to organization or business success. It is, therefore, essential to cultivate good relationships with others. To achieve this, you must learn how to talk, interact, and collaborate with others. Some of the aspects highlighted by Daniel Goleman that can help build your partnerships include:

• Self-reliance. This is the ability to think and reflect before acting. Self-reliance is essential when dealing with challenging circumstances or conflicts

• Internal motivation – this comes from within an individual. It refers to the ability to accomplish goals for personal reasons, not because there is a reward tied to it

- Understanding-refers to the ability to appreciate those around you, and also to motivate them. This is important for leaders who work with teams

- Social skills – the ability to form and manage relationships

Emotional Intelligence and The Workplace   Most experts consider EQ as one of the most valuable assets in the work environment. This is because employees with high EQ levels are better placed to manage stress, collaborate with their peers, and complete projects under minimal or no supervision.

Although high EQ is not essential for every workplace, every job that involves interaction with people requires emotionally intelligent staff. For instance, real estate or sales agents need individuals with good communication and negotiation skills. Individualistic jobs such as research and accounting do not necessarily require such skills. If knowledgeable employees are placed in positions where they need to work alone, they may underperform on the job since they would spend more time trying to reach out to other people than doing their job.

EQ And Leadership Skills

Although emotional intelligence can be optional for employees at subordinate levels, it is essential for leadership positions. For leaders to be efficient, they must be able to relate well with their people. Good leaders often create a healthy work environment where others feel appreciated, inspired, and essential.

Most emotionally intelligent leaders can build trust with their employees. They see each individual as a person with unique abilities, behaviors, and backgrounds. They do not treat teams as a uniform collective. They also recognize and associate with each team member's emotions by sharing their concerns and joys alike.

Building trust with other employees is essential when you have to introduce a new concept to them. If the team trusts you, it will be easy to convince them to try out something new since they have confidence in your leadership.

Just like any other relationships, workplace relationships may experience some misunderstandings here and there. When this happens, only emotionally intelligent leaders can resolve it amicably, ensuring that the involved parties remain in good terms.

Good leaders are always bold when it comes to admitting their mistakes. This way, they can easily progress work relations by allowing others to learn some EI skills. They will be able to train their brain by regularly practicing what they learn from you. Before long, they will turn this into a habit, and you will notice a change in their behavior.

A leader that has low EQ always finds it difficult to relate with others. He will not be useful in identifying the expectations and needs of those he is leading. A leader who allows an outburst of his emotions without controlling them can create mistrust and disrespect among subordinates. Such an action can harm the attitude, culture, and feeling of other staff towards the organization. Good leaders always understand how their communication, whether verbal or non-verbal, can affect the entire team.

How Does Emotional Intelligence Look Like on Leadership? According to Daniel Goleman, emotional intelligence can be identified in leaders by checking their behaviors. Some of the typical attributes include:

• Leading from the front. Being an example to the team. Inspiring them to focus on the common goal

• Confidence, consistency, and honesty. These are attributes of self-awareness

• Good communication skills. Emotionally intelligent leaders are easy to approach and confide in

• Straight forward, clear and intuitive when it comes to making decisions

• Empathy and influence

Chapter 5. Analize body language

Body language is a universal language, while inevitably there are some regional nuances. For the most part, you'll be able to appraise a person and read into their thoughts solely from their body displays. We're going to break down some of the ordinary, more applicable aspects of reading body language so that you're not bogged down with excessive, possibly useless information.

Context is key. A person will react to numerous stimuli in their vicinity. You have to be aware of the environment's changes or just the environment's status to know if your subject is reacting to you or an increased room temperature. As the detector, you have to keep track of the changes in the environment. You need to know if a light is flickering, it will be a distraction. You have to notice if the air has kicked in and it's getting colder in the room. Are there annoying sounds? Displeasing aesthetics? Anything and everything are essential.

Importance of the Environment The first exercise in learning body language is to notice the things going on around you. Start up a conversation with a person your intent on observing and make sure you see without missing parts of the conversation what is going on. Take a mental note if something changes so you can monitor the new baseline of behavior. If for instance, the air conditioner does kick on in the middle of your conversation with someone, take note of when it turns off again. Wait a few moments for things to baseline again, and then bring up the pervious parts of the conversation the person reacted to. If they rubbed their arms while they spoke, they may have been cold, but if they do it again and the temperature has started to warm up, it could be a sign of unease.

Learning a Baseline Any successful interrogator knows to establish a baseline with their suspect before moving towards taboo subjects that may cause discomfort. Once a baseline is established all future gestures and motions can be compared to a truthful, foundational display.

You may not fully be aware of the baseline behavior of even people that are close to you. So, take some time to start conversations with individuals and establish their personality and baseline. Take the conversation to multiple topics. Start with very neutral subjects, move to more passion invoking ones and happier ones back to neutral.

Once you've spent some time getting accustomed to changes in the environment and establishing a baseline, you're ready to start learning what the gestures you've been noticing mean.

Primitive Movements There are different kinds of body language. Most actions are conscious, meaning they can be faked or omitted at will. Real liars versed in the ways of deceit know this and use this to their advantage. Everyday citizens who may only lie on occasion to save face, may not be as well versed. That is where our advantage lies. We want to distinguish our usually loving co-worker's sudden interest in our project as a power play. Thankfully though, there are primitive reactions that happen subconsciously and are far more reliable some of the

gestures that can be faked. For the sake of diversity, we'll cover both.

Freeze, flight or fight? More often than not, a person will freeze to evaluate whether or not fight or flight is the appropriate reaction to their situation. It could be a splitsecond freeze, that happens just long enough for the perpetrator to send their brain a signal to unfreeze. Look for the freeze.

Have you ever caught a child sneaking into the proverbial, metaphorical cookie jar? If they even start to hear someone's footsteps they may freeze before they react in any other way. If you've caught them and you speak to announce your presence, they are sure to pause and they'll probably even turn around slowly to discover your presence.

Just as a child will pause when caught, a manipulator will pause. An average person lying may not think anything of their sudden freezing movement. Still, a full-fledged manipulator may only let the freeze last a split-second, may play the freeze off as a different reaction, or even try to convince you there was a freeze at all.

People don't just freeze for a physical threat; they freeze at thoughts. Have you ever paused suddenly in the middle of an action because you remembered something? The same will happen to a manipulator if they think they've been caught or if they think they are in danger of being discovered.

A form of flight. Often, when people feel threatened in some way, they will find ways to put distance between them and the negative stimuli or find a barrier. Distance can be achieved by merely taking a step back, leaning wholly or back existing the room/situation. If you notice a person depending back away from you while standing, they may be starting to feel threatened.

Continuing with the child metaphor, have you ever watched a child try to hide or sneak? What do they do? They either cover their eyes, thinking that if they can't see you, you can't see them, or they try to make themselves smaller. If they hunch over and walk past you, suddenly they are camouflaged and you can't see them – or so they hope. You can watch a child who has done something wrong try to exit the room hunched over. The same is true for adults who are trying to get away with lying, however, with time to grow up, adults tend to change how they hunch over.

While, an adult in trouble is just as likely to try to become a turtle: pull their shoulders up and forward and tuck their head down as the try to gaze towards the floor, there are also other displays of trying to hide.

Barriers. Other times, simple barriers will do. Have you ever noticed someone put their ankle on their knee, forming a table on their lap? The shin facing outward is a barrier. It's a form of keeping threats at bay. So, if you're having a sitting conversation with someone and you notice they start to lean back in their chair and prop their leg up to form a barrier between you and them, you may want to take note of the topic. While this may be a sign they disagree with your view, it could also be worth exploring the topic a little more, especially if you've already got the sense that something is off.

Some people may pick up objects to act as a barrier between you and them instead of changing their body position. The same way children have security blankets or stuffed animal they can press against their chest, lying adults may also want a security blanket of sorts. Pillows on couches are often grabbed, if there are no items, the arms could be placed across the chest.

Check the Feet. Just as looking at the bottom of someone's feet will tell you where they've been, looking at the feet' direction will tell you where they are going. While this phrase may seem obvious, looking at the direction someone's feet is pointing will say to you where they want to be. If a person is sitting on a couch, but have moved their feet to face the door, they may be ready to leave. This becomes especially true if they've moved their stance to prepare for standing up, like scooting towards the edge of the cushion and leaning forward, ready to shift their weight to their legs.

People can point their feet in the direction they want to go if they are uncomfortable and want to leave the current situation faster. Just like leaving the scene of a crime before the law enforcement shows up. While not everyone will want to flee the conversation because you've brought up something they may be lying about, some will especially if they can use leaving as an excuse not to have to talk about it. Leaving gives them more time to think of what to say, how to say it and how to come off as truthful or convince you it was all a misunderstanding.

Locking. Women are more prone to locking their legs or ankles because they've been taught to sit this way, especially when wearing a skirt. However, if a man interlocks his ankles while sitting, he displays a high stress level and should raise a red flag. For either gender, sudden locking of the ankles is a sign that something may be off. Prolonged ankle locking is a way of restricting movement.

Just as the freeze instinct suggestions, people tend to cease their movements when they are lying. If someone has been using gestures frequently and suddenly stops, this may indicate that they have started lying. If someone's feet have been moving regularly during a conversation, especially while sitting and they suddenly cease, take note.

Evolving Joe Navarro an FBI agent trained in interrogation states that after every primitive response, there will be a pacifying behavior. These behaviors are mechanisms to calm anxiety or fear. They are big discomfort flags.

Going for the Neck. The neck is the most prominent pacifying area. Men like to rub their necks, touch their collars or pull on their ties, women will play with necklaces, or touch around their collar bone and center of the neck.

Sometimes, when a woman puts her arms across her chest, she is cupping her right elbow with her left hand. When she does this, she puts a barrier between her and the person she is talking to. If things get uncomfortable, she will move her right hand to her neck. She may play with a necklace or touch her fingers to her neck to display her discomfort.

The Cleanser. The cleanser is a well-known sign of discomfort or stress. Have you ever noticed someone rubbing their hands, or more accurately, their palms down their thighs? This action can be done once or repetitiously depending on why the reaction is occurring. The cleanser could be used for two reasons, the person has started to sweat (possibly from anxiety) or is using it to alleviate. With either reasoning the cleanser is a behavior to notice. The subject may be more prone to use it if they think a table is blocking the view of their thighs and palms. An easy way to still notice the cleanser is to watch the elbows/arms and shoulders if their hands have disappeared under the table, you will even see a forward and backwards motion in these regions.

Chapter 6. Facial Expressions

Take into account your looks on the outside. Think about how much a person can pass on with just an external appearance. A smile may reflect happiness or approval. A fake smile can flag unhappiness or hopelessness. Our physical appearance can now and again show our specific feelings about a particular situation. While you're pretending, you're feeling fine the whole phrase could tell people something else. Some examples of emotions that can be conveyed through physical actions include:

⬛ Joy

⬛ gloomy

⬛ Getting angry

⬛ Shocked

⬛ Disgusting feeling

⬛ Anxiety

⬛ Feeling confused

⬛ Happiness

⬛ Aspiration

⬛ Contempt

A Scientist went on and found help for the completeness of several outward appearances linked to individual emotions, including euphoria, anger, fear, pain, and sadness. A study even suggests that we use their appearances and articulations to decide individuals' current knowledge. One study found that people with smaller faces and increasingly visible noses were expected to be deemed astute. Individuals with smiling, serene resonance were also selected to be more favorable than those with articulations of frustration. Physical attributes do the share of a lion's responsibility in transmitting data to the next man. A regular person will not be able to explore the legs or arms' non-verbal communication. However, almost everyone can see the sign shown on an individual's heart. Therefore, we must maintain a good and sufficient outward presentation if everyone hates us because we are not receptive. The critical articulation that everyone in a person is looking for is the smile. A smile can recover, but it can be not easy at the same time. A lady with a stiff-lipped smile that does not show any teeth is emblematic of her lack of enthusiasm for the debate. However, it may seem to an ordinary individual that she is charmed by the continuous conversation.

Real and Fake Smile There are numerous attributes of a unique grin. At whatever point individual usually grins, with no deliberate power, wrinkles are made around the eyes. This is because in a unique and real smile, the lip's corners are pulled up and the muscles around the eyes are contracted. In a phony grin, just lip developments occur. Individuals giving fake grins grin only through their mouth and not eyes. Imagine a scenario where the individual who you are conversing with attempts to deliver a phony grin by wrinkling their eyes willfully. There is a stunt to distinguish this too. At the point when a grin is veritable, the plump piece of the eye between the eyebrow and the eyelid moves descending and the parts of the bargains additionally plunge to a slight degree. Research has demonstrated that the more individual grins, the more

positive response he/she gets from the others. There is one all the more method to identify false grins. When an individual attempts to counterfeit a grin, the right side of the cerebrum's hemisphere – the one work in outward appearances sends flag just to one side of the body. Henceforth, a phony grin will consistently be more grounded on one side and more fragile on the opposite side. Be that as it may, in a certified grin, the two pieces of the cerebrum send signals and thus, the grin is similarly solid on both sides. If by any chance individual's eyes are turning away from you, at that point you should understand that the individual is exhausted from you and it is smarter to either change the subject of dialog or leave. Be that as it may, if the lips are marginally squeezed, the eyebrows are raised and there is a watchful eye of eyes at you alongside the head erect or somewhat pushed forward, at that point this suggests enthusiasm of the individual in you.

Eyes Eyes have such an enormous significance in any discussion or association that if the eyes' language turns out badly, the whole debate and the individual's notoriety turns out badly.

Eyes communicate in a language that is inevitable from others' eyes. Eye to eye connection manages discussion and clues about accommodation and strength also. What individuals see about another when they meet just because are the eyes. Also, subsequently, both the gatherings included make quick decisions about one another dependent on the eyes. Eyes are thus, the vehicle of passing on data about other individuals' frames of mind and contemplations. Give us a chance to take a gander at a portion of the messages passed on by the eyes.

The Dilating and Contracting of Pupils When somebody gets energized, the students get expanded and can widen up to multiple times the first size. On the other hand, when an individual is furious or in some other negative state of mind, the understudy's contract. Thus, if you find that the other individual's students have enlarged, it implies the individual is keen on you or in your discussion. In any case, if the understudies have contracted, at that point, it is smarter to comprehend that the individual isn't intrigued.

The Flash of the Eyebrow In pretty much every culture, a long separation "hi" is passed on by the eyebrow's brisk ascent and fall. This is called as the eyebrow streak or flash. The brief instant development of the eyebrow is a method for welcome one another. It has a contrary undertone in Japan and must not be utilized with individuals from Japan.

The Eyebrows Game The rise of your eyebrows during discussion suggests accommodation. Then again, the bringing down of eyebrows connotes predominance. Those individuals who deliberately cause a rise in their eyebrows seem compliant, and the individuals who lower their eyebrows are commonly viewed as forceful.

There is one trick here. When women bring down their eyelids and cause a rise in their eyebrows simultaneously, it passes on sexual accommodation. This articulation must, henceforth, be kept away from informal and professional workplaces.

It is prescribed continuously that an individual must keep in touch with the other individual to show a degree of intrigue and expectation. Be that as it may, if you continue taking a gander at the other individual for quite a while, it might put the other individual at some inconvenience. Your look might threaten the other individual. In many societies, it has been discovered that to construct a decent affinity with the other individual, your look must meet the other individual's look for about 60% to 70% of the time. If you continue looking at them with intrigue, different individuals will feel that you like them and subsequently, they will also respond with their look. In any case, if you find that the other individual isn't taking a look at you for a specific timeframe and is somewhat turning away from you regularly, at that point the discussion needs to end or the subject of the debate needs to change. If you are uncertain of to what extent you should glance at the other individual, the most secure wager is to take a look at the other individual for the time the person is taking a look at you. Turning away during a cross-examination likewise gives away the signal that the individual is lying.

The Sideways Glance   The sideways look can be seen as a declaration of intrigue or even threatening vibe. When a sideways look is joined with a grin or somewhat caused a commotion, it can convey intrigue and an acclaimed romance sign. Notwithstanding, if the sideways look is bound with a grimace, downturned eyebrows, and downturned lips, it can pass on doubt, analysis, or even antagonistic vibe.

The Blinking Magic The rate at which your eyes squint is additionally a transport of essential data. If you are keen on somebody's discussion, you won't flutter your eyelid as frequently. Be that as it may, on the off chance that somebody does not inspire you, your pace of squinting the eyes will increment drastically. Increment in the squinting pace of the eyes passes on a lack of engagement or fatigue.

The Dart If the other individual's eyes start to shoot from one side to the next, it suggests that the individual has lost enthusiasm for you and is searching for break courses to be away from you. This uncovers the other individual's instability.

The Authority Gaze One approach to radiate authority is to bring down your eyebrows, slender the eyelids, and spotlight the other individual intently. This gives an impression of what predators do right before assaulting their prey. The flickering rate needs to diminish and there must be a consistent spotlight on the other individual's eyes.

Eye-to-eye connection and eye developments are a significant part of our relational abilities and our non-verbal communication. Thus, it is of most extreme significance to keep in touch with the other individual, without threatening that person. Eye to eye connection assumes a critical job in deals interviews, prospective employee meetings, and easygoing discussions.

Fingers Regardless of whether the eyes, arms, and legs are at a legitimate spot, the fingers can in any case play as a spoiler. The hands and the fingers together give away a great deal of data about us and different individuals. Besides, when we talk with our hand signals and finger developments, it is simpler for the other individual to hold what we have spoken about. Thus, hand developments help in the maintenance of messages as well. Give us a chance to investigate the distinctive hand motions that are regularly seen in the world over.

Scouring of Palms The scouring of palms against one another is seen to be an indication of hope. Scouring of palms together is representative of having the desire for positive results. This articulation is very regular in deals pitch also. The business groups of numerous associations advise about an idea to other individuals utilizing collapsed hands and palms scouring against one another.

Scouring the palms faster shows that the individual is thinking about the other's advantages and is an amicable individual. On the other hand, a moderate rub of hands with a grin passes on insidious aims and the individual is narrowminded.

Thumb and Finger Rub   The scouring of fingers and the thumb against one another shows that the individual hopes to get cash. This is one motivation behind why this signal must be utilized with an alert before individuals

Chapter 7. Microexpressions

Microexpressions are a particular category of facial expressions, considerable and specific scientific research during the past fifty years. We define microexpressions as subtle muscular movements in the face with a duration of half a second or less. Microexpressions often occur unconsciously and reflect emotions that we are feeling at that particular moment. If you compare the face to a screen, the brain is the projector of our feelings, which cause our facial muscles to contract for just a brief instant.

Seven basic emotions are shown in the same way in the face in all cultures. Research conducted among blind people has proven that microexpressions are not culturally learned, but are biological phenomena that each of us is equipped with from birth. They are the physical reaction to the way our brain translates emotional impulses. What's more, most people cannot control these muscles' unconscious contractions because the emotions directly generate them.

Microexpressions display most of the basic emotions. Robert Plutchik was the first to develop the theory of eight basic emotions: sorrow, dislike, anger, fear, anticipation, pleasure, acceptance, and surprise. He even developed a specific graphic in color for each emotion to reflect that they could be combined to create new feelings; for example, fear + surprise = alarm or pleasure + fear = guilt. Since it was impossible to observe anticipation and acceptance as a universal code visible in the face, the only positive emotion that remained in Plutchik's theory was pleasure, later more commonly referred to as happiness. This term covers a whole family of positive emotions, including acceptance, anticipation, approval, pleasure, and joy.

Today, microexpressions are grouped into seven basic and universal emotions: anger, dislike, fear, surprise, happiness, sadness, and contempt.

We now refer to as microexpressions first identified in the nineteenth century by Duchenne de Boulogne, a famous French neurologist. He combined his vast knowledge of facial anatomy with his passion for photography and his expertise in using electricity to stimulate individual muscles

in the face. He recorded his conclusion in his book The Mechanism of Human Facial Expression, published in 1862.

The second person to write about microexpressions was Charles Darwin in The Expression of the Emotions in Man and Animals, published in 1872. Darwin noted the universal nature of facial expressions and listed the muscles that were used to generate them. In their 1966 study findings, Haggard and Isaacs reported how they had been able to observe "micro-moment facial expressions" when examining films of psychotherapy sessions, initially searching for signals of nonverbal communication between therapists and their patients. Ekman and Friesen conducted numerous investigations into facial expressions. They were eventually able to confirm that seven basic emotions are displayed facially in the same manner in twenty-one different cultures.

In 1960, William S. Condon conducted pioneering research into interactions that last for fractions of a second. He reduced his groundbreaking conclusions to a film fragment lasting just four and a half seconds. Each of the constituent images he had analyzed and recorded lasted for only 1/25 of a second. After examining this film fragment minutely for eighteen months, he reported what he called "interactional

micro-movements"; for example, how a woman raised her shoulder at almost the same moment as a man raised his hand. According to Condon, this interplay of micromovements combined made possible a series of microrhythms.

Paul Ekman's later research into emotions and their relationship to facial expressions took Darwin's work to a higher level. They proved beyond question that certain emotion-related facial expressions are not culturally determined, but are biological in origin. These expressions are universal and transcend cultures.

Based on his work, in 1976 Ekman developed his Facial Action Coding System (FACS) with Wallace V. Freisen. FACS is a system for classifying human facial expressions and is still used today by psychologists, researchers, and animators.

we look at the most common variations of three of the seven basic emotions, which can occur regularly in day-to-day conversation. If you have already had microexpression training, you will notice that our approach to identifying and interpreting short muscular movements in the face is designed to make things as simple as possible. This is because we refer to all facial expressions of half a second or

less by the generic term microexpressions, even though from a purely scientific perspective some of them can better be described as partial expressions, subtle expressions, or masked expressions. While there are slight differences between the different types of partial, subtle, and masked expressions.

Neutral Face

1. The Neutral Face Is Your Basis for Comparison.

It is essential to identify when someone is wearing a neutral face. This gives you a basis for comparing or noticing the difference when the facial microexpressions activated by emotions kick in.

Sometimes, wearing a neutral look may express that the person is experiencing no feelings at that

particular moment or has no opinion about what she is hearing. It can be useful to check if she is paying attention to what you are saying in such situations. She is always possible to simply not listen to you or have not adequately heard what you said.

You have probably experienced when someone deliberately puts on a poker face. Most of us are capable of producing our variant of this, when necessary. For this reason, it is essential to be able to make a distinction between a neutral face and a poker face. A neutral face will appear more relaxed and more spontaneous than a poker face. With a poker face, you often get the impression that the person concerned is wearing a mask. The muscles in the face are more tensed and you can notice that the person is deliberately trying to suppress reactions to what is happening around him. He will not answer questions spontaneously, but will first take time to think about how he wants to respond, while at the same time attempting not to react with his face.

This is also why people with something to hide often wear dark sunglasses, so that people cannot see part of their face and, in particular, their eyes.

Happiness: Corners of the Mouth Turned Up You can read happiness in someone's face when both corners of their mouth are turned up symmetrically to the same level. If you can recognize it, this microexpression is extremely useful in everyday life. For example, if I ask my partner what she wants to do tonight, "Shall we meet up with friends, stay at home, or go to the movies?" and if I see both corners of her mouth turn up when I mention friends, then I know that she has already made her nonverbal choice.

Both Corners of The Mouth Turned Up Indicate Happiness.

Compare This with a Real, Wholehearted Smile of Joy

This is not a microexpression, but we show it as an example to see the difference between a microexpression that lasts for

half a second or less and a microexpression that lasts for significantly longer. The photo is also useful to see the difference between a real and a false smile.

When you see the orbicularis oculi (the muscle around the eye) contract, you know that you are looking at a real smile, a so-called Duchenne smile. The orbicularis oculi muscles' contraction makes the skin areas between the eyes and the outer edge of the eyebrows stretch and lower slightly, often accompanied by the slight lowering of the eyebrows. These two movements are a reliable indicator that someone is experiencing pleasure in the left prefrontal cortex of their brain, so that the happiness they are expressing is genuine.

This Is Not a Microexpression.

How Good Are People at Recognizing Microexpressions?

When people first do a microexpression test, the average score is 24.09 percent (based on 2,664 unique test results worldwide in 2012). Fewer than 12 percent achieve a score of more than 50 percent. This concludes that most people pay little attention to microexpressions in their daily conversations. Otherwise, they are not aware of the significance of these small muscular contractions, which are nevertheless the most reliable indicators of the way people are feeling.

Chapter 8. The art of persuasion

What comes to your mind when you think about this question? Some think it is creating a desperate message to buy a product, while others believe it tries to influence voters. The problem is a powerful force in everyday life, which has a significant impact on security. Decisions' power and control influence policies, legal decisions, media, news, and insights. At times, we want to believe that we are not affected by persuasion. We have the natural ability to look at this sale, recognize the situation's truth, and make our own decisions. This may be true in some scenarios, but it is not necessarily the seller trying to convince you, or a TV commercial asking you to buy the latest and greatest item. Persuasion can be subtle, and there can be many factors in how we try to gain influence.

According to Perloff (2003), influence can be defined as a symbolic process in which communicators try to persuade other people to change their perspectives or behaviors

regarding an issue by transmitting a message in an atmosphere of free choice.

The Main Reasons for this Definition are:

• It is recommended to use words, photos, sounds, etc.

• This is an explanation to influence others.

• Persuasion is useful. No one found the choice is yours.

• How to provide a particular action in different cases, including verbal, unnecessary, dissemination, and information.

How Is It Different Today? Art and the method we chose accurately determined the ancient Grecques' times, but there are significant differences shown in the past. In his book "The Dynamics of Belief: Communication and Attitudes in the 21st Century, Richard

M. Perlov describes the five most important questions that new questions are different from others.

The number of persuasive measures has increased significantly. For a moment, think about how many you can find each day. To ensure the number of times the US results are reached, it ranges from about 300 to over 3,000. Make sure the communication is quick. This is the reason, and the intent to spread it very quick. Persuasion is a business that companies (distributors, companies, public companies, etc.) only operate for a specific purpose.

Persuasion is not trivial. Of course, few ads use very compelling strategies, but many messages are much more subtle. For example, a particular schedule may be set very precisely to plan for product purchase or life extension. The question is more complicated. As customers are more identifiable and make more decisions, they need to determine when they can persuade compelling media and messages.

Modern persuasion : Pratkans & Aron (1991) states that some companies make better decision than others. In contrast to communication

that controls transactions, the right choices are left to the advertisers. Discussions are raised in response to the authority, not by or in the power of the administration. Rules are chosen based on their ability, not the royal family, but one of the biggest reasons. Good looking and behaving candidates almost always win.

The old Greeks had a better approach to making decisions. The Greeks, who are stationed, can hire an employee to protect him. The hiking teachers and writers probably decided to know-you can say they were the best students in the world. Sophists argued that a persuasion is a tool that helps find the truth. They thought that the discussion and the reason for the debate would generate good ideas and allow good ideas to come back. It did not matter what problem he was working on. Sophists would have been in the middle of discussions for some time. The stated goals of them have been confirmed that the truth has been resolved. They believed in the free practice of good ideas.

Does it sound like our world? No, we are leveraging success, and we can state that this is more than an opportunity did. But what is the modern approach to answering the question of whether it is right or wrong? Of course. It is essential to

reach the masses "through the manipulation of symbols and most of us human emotions." to achieve their goals, I think that subject is taught at school because the ability to ask and examine questions is directly related to someone's success in life. I think they know the right tactics as much as they know the letters of the alphabet and the right way, or how to improve CPR.

But how can we reflect the ten principles of belief? How many of us can find the situation and the right tool for the job? How many people know the times when someone is influenced by someone every day? Do this: Take a look at your decision, or your pantry, or your organization. Everyone you see is a trophy that represents some of the companies that exceed their goals. For some reason, or perhaps no reason at all, they may allow you to make your money on your products. Many influencing factors play a role in our security. They are at the top of your business and thrive by letting you think, do what you want, and get it done.

Most people are unaware of these effects or, if they are, overestimate the amount of freedom needed to realize their thoughts. But we know that a strong influence is a question

that will help your decision to determine his approach if he can handle the situation and choose the right method.

Methods of Persuasion: The ultimate goal of persuasion is to persuade one to internalize the right argument and adopt that new attitude as part of the decision. Below are just a few of the most effective ways to influence. Other methods include rewards, positive or negative experiences, and many other uses.

Create your Needs: One way of identifying is to create the needs you need. This kind of exam is a fundamental pre-requisite for whether it is a matter of self-determination and self-realization. Manufacturers often use this method to solve problems. For example, think about how many suggestions you need to find a particular product and make sure it is good.

Addressing Social Needs: It is another very effective method that appeals to the need to be popular, and renowned. Television ads provide many examples of these types of questions. It is essential to buy

these questions to look like a known or familiar person. Television is a big challenge to convince people.

Use Old Words and Photos: It is also widely used for using loaded words and images. Advocates will notice the power of positive words that frequently use phrases such as "new and improved" or "allnatural."

Put Your Foot in the Door: It is also ineffective to get people to meet their requirements, known as the "get it started" technique. It is essential to ask a question to answer a small question, such as asking a small question to be answered by creating the query. By having a person accept the first favor, the applicant is more likely to "feel," and that person is more likely to agree with the more extensive requirements. For example, a neighbor has asked you to babysit two children for one or two. If you agree, ask if you can ask your child for the rest of the time.

You have always chosen smaller requirements, so you might feel the obligation to face larger ones. This is an excellent example of what applies to approval rules, and we

recommend that you use this method to encourage consumers to buy your product.

Increase and then Decrease: This approach is different from the foot-in-the-door approach. Specific questions often start with making unnecessary requests. A person responds by rejecting the door for sale and figuratively blaming it. The answer to this question is to create a much smaller requirement that is often considered invalid. Feel the obligation to meet these offers. Since they rejected this initial request, they often help answer small requests.

Harness the Power of Security: When you have someone in you, it can be overwhelming to bring your family back kindly. It is known as a kind of correctness. Someone did something for you, so a particular obligation to do something for someone. Manufacturers can use this method to give kindness, including "extras" and making decisions to force offers or purchases.

Create another Point for Innovation: Decisions are subtle cognitive biases that can impact diet and decisions. If you try to reach a decision, the first offer tends to decide for all future decisions. Therefore, if you try to propose a number first and try to negotiate for a particular question, it can affect future negotiations in your life, especially if the number is a little higher. This first number is the correct point. You may not get it, but a high start can lead to higher offers from your employer.

Limit Availability: Robert Cardin's decision is known for six principles that influence the fact that it is best explained in his most decisive influence in 1984 on influence. One of the keys he identified is known to be secure or to limit the availability of something.

He suggested that situations improve when things are scared or limited. We would buy something if they believed it was the last one or it would be there soon. For example, the answer could only be a limited run of a particular print. Only some printouts are available, so you may decide before you leave.

Spend Time Realizing that you have a Question: Examples are just a few of the main persuasion techniques described by certain psychologists. Look for persuasive examples in your daily life. An interesting experiment is to revisit the 30 minutes of a particular schedule and write down a compelling assessment of all kinds. With a certain number of techniques used in a short time, you may be surprised.

Chapter 9. Mental manipulation

Manipulation is where individuals will work to get what they want, often using hidden and underhand tricks. They see the other person in the relationship (whether it is a romantic relationship, familiar relationship, friendship, or someone at work) only as a tool that they can use to get their way. They often don't care if they end up harming the other person in the process or not, as long as they get what they want.

Different types of manipulation are sometimes used to an agreement or help someone mutually beneficial to both parties. But when it comes to dark psychology, manipulation helps just the manipulator and no one else in the process. Many techniques can be used with manipulation—including foot in the door, intimidation, lying, love bombing, and more.

In dark psychology, the dark triad is often going to talk about psychopathy, Machiavellianism, and narcissism. These will be known as dark traits because of some of the evil parts that

go with them. Research on these traits is used in a field known as applied psychology—especially when we are looking into business management, clinical psychology, and law enforcement. People who test for and then end up scoring high on these kinds of traits are the most likely to commit crimes, cause trouble in society, and create problems inside a business if hired, especially when they land a leadership role.

All three of these dark traits will be conceptually distinct from one another, although evidence shows that they easily will overlap sometimes. They are going to be associated with a personality type that is very manipulative and callous towards others, which can make it hard for them to have close friends or anyone at all who wants to do something with them at any time.

To help us understand these a bit more and see what the personality traits are all about and why we want to mention them in dark psychology.

Machiavellianism The first trait of the dark triad that we will take a look at is known as Machiavellianism. The trait was first given name

after the political philosophy promoted by Niccolò Machiavelli. If someone scores high with this kind of trait, they will be very cynical, which means that they will be skeptical of others and be more interested in the self than others, even in an unethical way.

Also, scoring high with this kind of personality trait will mean that the person is dishonest and cold. They believe that the way to success is interpersonal manipulation with pretty much everyone they meet, and because of these thoughts, they are going to act accordingly.

This kind of person has an idea of what they want in life, and they don't care what it is going to take to get that thing. If they have to walk all over people, manipulate others, and cause trouble, they will do it. Keeping up with what they will do next to get what they want is going to be hard.

Narcissism The next thing that we need to take a look at is the idea of narcissism. Individuals who end up scoring high with this particular trait will display a lot of superiority, dominance, entitlement, and grandiosity in everything they do. With this one, you will run across someone who doesn't even

comprehend that other people have feelings and thoughts, and they act in the manner they do because of this misunderstanding.

To the narcissist, other people are simply tools that they can use for their benefit. They don't care whether the other person is hurt on the way to success, and often they assume that others think and react to the world in the same way that they do. They will often hold onto their target for a long time because it allows them to do what they want without searching for another person to give them constant praise and attention. But since they have no care for how the other person is treated, this target will mostly end up with mental and emotional problems if they stay in the relationship for an extended period.

Psychopathy Compared to the other two parts of this triad, psychopathy will be seen as the three's evilest. Individuals who score high on this kind of issue will show very low empathy levels and higher thrill-seeking and impulsivity levels. This means that when a psychopath wants something, they want to do it right now, and they don't have much care for the thoughts or

feelings of the other people around them at all. Often, this will be even lower than what we would see with the other two options.

Researchers have found a similarity that shows up between those with antisocial personality disorder and psychopathy, so this will need to be explored more in the future. This is seen as one of the worst conditions out of the three, and without proper care, it can cause a lot of issues along the way with interpersonal relationships.

The dark triad can cause many workplace problems, in society, and in any relationship that becomes a part of it. They may be in love with the dark psychologist and want to see what it takes to make things work, but often, the dark psychologist has no want or need to make things right. As long as the target continues doing what they should, even when the target gets hurt, the dark psychologist will keep on with the same course of action, getting what they want in the process.

Mind Control It is a system of influences that come into play to disrupt the individual on a significant level. The hope is to shake up the individual so much that you can get to their core and change up their identity, putting in a brand-new identity in its place, one that the manipulator will design to fit their needs.

It can sometimes be used in beneficial ways. Some mind control techniques help change the addict's personality and help them get over their addiction. But here, we will take a look more at the uses of mind control that force the individual to change to benefit the manipulator, not anything that will benefit the target.

According to a psychologist known as Philip Zimbardo, mind control will be the process where the individual action and choice will be compromised by agents or agencies trying to modify things like cognition, affect, motivation, perception, and behavioral outcomes. And it is believed that everyone, no matter who they are and their background, could be susceptible at some point to this manipulation.

With mind control, it will not be some ancient mystery that only a few people know about. It will be a combination of words and even group pressures that makes the manipulator create dependency on those who use it. The manipulator will gain full control and make decisions for those they control, while the target assumes that they still have the freedom to decide. This is part of mind control; the target is not aware of the influence process or even its changes.

There are techniques you can use to execute some influence over other people around you. And often, when you are using these with the ideas of dark psychology, you are planning on using them to gain your benefit without worrying about how it can influence or harm another person.

Persuasion Persuasion is something that we experience daily. We are going to be persuaded by friends and family to help out on occasion. We will see many advertisements from companies that want to convince us to purchase their products and not from competitors. We see persuasion so often that it is sometimes hard to realize that it could be harmful and that a manipulator could try to use this against us.

When it comes to persuasion, Robert Cialdini is well respected for some of his ideas on persuasion and how to do it successfully, whether your intentions are good or not.

According to Cialdini, six principles can be used to help out with the ideas of persuasion, and these six principles are going to include:

Reciprocity: This is where you will do a small favor for someone, and then right away, ask them to do one back.

Commitment and consistency: It hold the target of doing something because they have done it in the past.

Social proof: This is when you convince the target to do something because it is popular, and everyone is doing it.

Authority: Your target is more likely to do something if they believe you are an authority on that topic.

Likeability: If you can become likable and see you as a friend, they are more likely to do what you ask.

Scarcity: This is the fear that an item will be in short supply, so they want to get it.

There are persuasive techniques to get hold of your target and get them to do what you want while they still believe they have full control over their thoughts and actions at this time.

Deception Another technique that a dark psychologist can use is known as deception. This will refer back to the act, whether it is kind or cruel or big or small, of causing another person, your target, to believe something that is not true. Even those who are pretty honest will practice this deception at some time, and it is believed that the average person will lie at least a few times a day, even if the lies are not significant and won't harm the other person.

There are many ways to lie about things to the other person, but it is usually to hide some information from the target to react in the manner that the manipulator wants. This makes sure that the target will respond the way the manipulator wants without really knowing why it would be the wrong decision. The manipulator gets what they want because they

told an outright lie or hid some information, and often the target will be hurt in the process because of this.

Chapter 10.Types of Emotional manipulators

You've likely experienced individuals who are manipulative emotionally and controlling.

They utilize these practices to get their direction or prevent you from saying or doing anything they don't care for.

Emotional manipulation can be unpretentious and misleading, leaving you befuddled and wobbly.

Or then again, it tends to be clear and requesting where fears, disgracing, and remorseful fits leave you shocked and immobilized.

In any case, emotional manipulation isn't worthy, and the more you enable it to proceed, the more force and certainty the manipulator gains in this uneven relationship.

Inevitably, any leftover of a sound association is pulverized, as the establishment of trust, closeness, regard, and security disintegrates under the sled of manipulation.

a. Specific Types of Emotional Manipulation

Within these major categories of emotional manipulation techniques, psychologists have also identified a wide range of more subtle variations that we all likely encounter daily.

These techniques include:

- Lying: Dark Triad personalities, particularly psychopaths, are highly skilled at lying and cheating, so often we may not detect their intent until it is too late. Beware of those who have demonstrated a pattern of dishonesty.

- Lying by omission: Lying by omission is a little more subtle. The predator may not say anything untrue but may withhold information necessary to cause you to fail.

- Denial: Often the damage from emotional manipulation is inflicted after the fact. When you confront someone with evidence of their dishonesty and abuse, their refusal to admit wrongdoing can cause even more significant psychological harm.

- Rationalization: The increase in popular news media has led to public relations and marketing firms who produce "spin" to deflect criticism in political and corporate environments. Rationalization is a form of spin, in which a manipulator explains away his or her abuse.

- Minimization: Like rationalization, minimization is a form of denial in which the predator understates his or her offense's seriousness.

- Selective attention and/or inattention: Manipulators will pick and choose which parts of an argument or debate should be considered so that only their views are represented.

- Diversion: Manipulators often resist giving straight answers to questions, particularly when their victim confronts them. Instead, they will divert the conversation to some other topic or change the subject altogether.

- Evasion: More severe than diversion, a manipulative person confronted with his or her guilt will often completely evade responsibility by using long rambling responses filled with so-called "weasel words," like "most people would say," "according to my sources," or other phrases that falsely legitimize their excuses.

- Covert intimidation: Many manipulative people will make implied threats to discourage further inquiries or resolution.

- Guilt tripping: A proper form of emotional manipulation, a manipulator will exploit the integrity and conscientiousness of the victim by accusing them of being too selfish, too irresponsible, or not caring enough.

- Shaming: Although shaming can be used to bring about social change when large corporations or governments advance abusive or discriminatory policies, manipulators may attempt to intimidate their victims by using sharp

criticism, sarcastic comments, or insults to make them feel bad.

- Blaming the victim: This tactic has become increasingly common. When a victim accuses a predator of abuse, the predator will attempt to turn it around by creating a scenario in which the victim alone is responsible for the harm that came to him.

- Playing the victim: Using the opposite tactic of blaming the victim, the predator will lure a conscientious person into a trap by pretending to have been grievously wounded and cultivating feelings of sympathy. However, the real plan is to take advantage of the conscientious person's caring nature by conveying their emotions.

- Playing the servant: This tactic is common in environments marked by a strict, well-established chain of command, like the military. Predators become skilled at manipulating this system by creating a persona of suffering and nobility, in which their evil actions are justified as duty, obedience, and honor.

- Seduction: This technique does not always have to involve sexual conquest or intimacy. Emotional predators

may use flattery and charm to convince people to do their bidding, and they often look for people with low self-esteem.

- Projection: This term is used in psychotherapy. Predators who use this technique will look for victims to use as scapegoats. When the manipulator does something wrong and is confronted, they will "project" their guilt onto the victim to make them look like the responsible party.

- Feigning innocence: This technique can be used as part of a strategy of denial. Under questioning, the manipulator will "play innocent" by pretending that any violation was unintentional or that they were not the party who committed the offense.

- Feigning confusion: This technique can also be used as part of a strategy of denial. The manipulator will "play dumb" or pretend to be confused about the conflict or dispute's central point under questioning. By creating confusion, the manipulator hopes to damage the confidence of his or victim.

● Peer pressure: Using claims, whether true or not, that the victim's friends, associates, or "everyone else" is doing

something, the manipulator will put pressure on his victim to change his or her behavior or attitude.

b. Signs That You're Being Manipulated

We are all potentially susceptible to emotional manipulation by people who show characteristic signs of dark psychology.

A straightforward example can be Victimization: it can occur in our everyday relationships with co-workers, bosses and supervisors, family members, and significant others.

Emotional manipulation can also occur in professional relationships with people we may regard as usually trustworthy—such as sales representatives, government officials, and other representatives of institutions such as medical facilities, banks, businesses, schools, and law firms.

Emotional predators share one common trait: They look for conscientious, dependable, loyal, honest, and reliable. People with these character traits are the easiest to manipulate because all of the tricks in the manipulator's toolbox are explicitly designed to take advantage of these emotional and psychological characteristics. More importantly, emotional predators lack empathy or morality. They do not regard their abuses as shocking or unacceptable; instead, they consider the overabundance of conscientious people as "job security" and a golden opportunity.

Emotional predators can be found in all walks of life. Throughout their lives, they have learned how to adapt, blend in, and even achieve high levels of professional and financial success in the "straight world."

Remember that having a reasonable and legitimate expectation that people will be honest in their dealings with you means that you are a conscientious person. Although you occupy the superior position, emotional predators are highly skilled at exploiting this expectation and avoiding detection and/or punishment.

As we have seen, emotionally manipulative people use various techniques and methods to gain power in relationships. What's more, the people you are closest to and most familiar with— people whom you should be able to trust the most—are in the best position to use emotional manipulation to exploit and take advantage of your trust. Establishing trust and familiarity is one of the most important aspects of a successful effort to exploit someone's

emotional vulnerability, then manipulate them either for personal gain or simply out of pure malice.

Of course, simply because this type of abuse has become common does not mean that you should automatically and necessarily regard all of your friends and trusted associates as predators and manipulators. Nor should you give into the temptation to consider being conscientious, law-abiding, and honest as a problem. However, victims of emotional manipulation are often unaware that they are being exploited and abused, so it is crucial to learn how to recognize the signs of manipulation.

c. Specific Examples of Emotional Manipulation

• insisting on meeting at certain locations: Manipulators may try to get the upper hand by pressing on a so-called "home court advantage," thereby forcing you to function in a less familiar and less comfortable environment that diminishes your personal negotiating power.

Examples: o   If you have a dispute with a professional acquaintance or colleague, they may insist on always meeting in their office or

at a café or restaurant that is more difficult for you to travel to.

• Premature intimacy or closeness: The manipulator will immediately shower you with affection and reveal all sorts of intimate secrets.

Examples: o   In a personal relationship, the manipulator may introduce themselves using phrases like, "No one has ever made me feel like this before. I know we were made for each other."

• Managing conversations by always requiring you to speak first: In professional relationships, this is commonly used as a sales and negotiation technique to mine you for your information to make a more lucrative sale.

Examples: o   A salesperson may say something like, "Rather than bore you with details about our products or services, why don't you tell me about yourself and how you think we can help you?"

• Distorting or twisting facts: Whether in personal or professional relationships, manipulators will use conversational techniques to distort facts to make you doubt yourself and back down.

Example: o   A manipulator may use a phrase like, "I understand how you feel. I'd be angry, too. But the truth is, I never made that comment. I don't think your memory of that conversation is accurate. I know what you meant to say was that..."

• Intellectual bullying: An emotional manipulator may use an unnecessarily large volume of statistics, jargon, or other types of factual evidence to impose a sense of expertise.

- Bureaucratic bullying: This technique is similar to intellectual bullying. Unfortunately, this technique may indicate that someone is abusing their position of authority by insisting on placing as many obstacles, red tape, or other impediments in the way of what should be a straightforward resolution.

Example:

o Such a person may make a statement such as, "I understand your concerns, but I would encourage you not to pursue this any further. You have a legitimate complaint, but the expenses and time required will likely cost more than you will get in return.

- Passive aggression

There are many examples of passive aggressive behavior in conversation in both personal and professional relationships to force you to back down to the predatory efforts.

Examples: o A manipulator may try to make you feel bad for voicing your concerns by saying something along the lines of, "I understand that you are voicing an important objection, but have ever stopped to consider what will happen to the rest of the team if you eventually get your way?"

- Insults and put-downs: Manipulators are good at following up rude or mean-spirited comments with sarcasm or some other attempt at humor to make it seem like they were joking.

Example:

o "I know you worked hard on that presentation. It's too bad you wasted your time, though. But, hey, no worries. I'm sure it will be great preparation when you interview for your position."

Chapter 11. Character Traits of a Manipulator

How a manipulative person's mind works, is most likely only something a manipulative person could comprehend. The rest of us think about in confusion, wondering why or how someone could behave this way. Though, in some small way, we can all be a little manipulative at times. For example, most people will be willing to bend the truth, or omit information, on the odd occasion. For much the same reasons, such as trying to get others to do something for them or even to get permission for something. Trying to convince someone of your argument or get them to come around to your way of thinking, is a natural and evolutionary process. Pinker and Bloom (1990) claimed that we evolved to use language because it helped us adapt to our environments.

The use of language to manipulate others to help us is the evolutionary adaptation, appears to be a natural process. Why then, do some individuals influence others for more pervasive means? Not for survival or evolutionary means,

but purely for their own selfish needs. If they cannot achieve this control, they feel helpless and lack any agency in their lives. Why? Are they evil, are they unkind, are they born that way? Some might say it is a personality disorder that is bordering on a narcissistic level.

We will all try to persuade someone at some point in our lives, but we are not all narcissists. Whatever the reason for our attempts at persuasion, we usually want to remain on good terms with the person we are trying to manipulate. Not so for those who manipulate to control.

Kier Harding, a lead Mental Health practitioner, wrote a relevant article in The Diagnosis of Exclusion. He argued that those diagnosed with a personality disorder are people who are not very good at manipulating. Their attempts tend to be forceful and over exaggerated. Whereas a skillful manipulator will aim to persuade someone less overtly. They are not very good at it, which makes them unlikable characters with poor interpersonal skills. Usually also with a low self-esteem because of their background in life. This could be an argument indicating that controlling manipulators are from dysfunctional backgrounds.

How Then Can We Recognize Such A Deviant Person?

Common Traits Use of Language We have shown how powerful language can be, as an excellent tool of persuasion. There is more to the manipulative controller though than mere words. They will use tactics that mislead and unbalance their target's inner thoughts. We now understand that through language, they will:

• Use mistruths to mislead and confuse their target's regular thinking pattern.

• Force their target to decide speed, so they don't have time to analyze and think.

• Overwhelmingly talk to their target, making them feel small.

• Criticize their target's judgment so they begin to lose their selfesteem.

• Raise the tone of their voice and not be afraid to use aggressive body language.

• Ignore their target's needs, they are only interested in getting what they want and at any cost.

Invasion of Personal Space Most of us set boundaries around ourselves without realizing we are doing so. It is a kind of unspoken rule to protect our private space, such as not sitting so close that you are touching another person, especially a stranger. A manipulative character cares nothing about overstepping such boundaries. Whether this is because they do not understand, or they do not care is unclear. Initially, they are unlikely to invade their target's personal space. They will seek to build up a good rapport first. This shows that they understand boundaries because once they gain their target's confidence, they will ignore them.

Fodder for Thought Manipulators tend to be very ego-centric, with limited social skills. Their only concern is for themselves. Everything they

do in life will be about how it affects them, not how their actions affect others. Does this mean that they have a psychopathic disorder?

Take empathy for instance. Controlling manipulators are unlikely ever to show compassion. Empathy is a natural human emotion that aids in our survival techniques. A study by Meffert et al. indicates that those with a psychopathic disorder can control empathetic emotions. They lack sympathy of any kind because another weakness is simply another tool for them. When they detect any weakness in their target's resolve or personality, they will exploit it. The consequences to their victim are of little importance. The targets weakness's feed the manipulator's strength, making them bolder and often crueler in their actions.

Creating Rivalry Another tactic of the controlling manipulator is backstabbing. They may tell you how great a person you are to your face, making themselves look good. Behind your back, they are busy spreading malicious gossip and untruths about you.

This is a classic trait of a controlling manipulator as it creates a rivalry between people. Then, they can pick sides that will make them look favorable, particularly to their

target. It can act as the first stage to getting close to their target. Once bonded, they can build up trust, making it easier to manipulate the target in the future. If you recognize a backstabber, keep them at a distance. Their plan is selfish so it is better not let them into your personal life. There is no point treating them as they treat you, in revenge. It will turn out to be exhausting playing them at their own game. If they know that you are on to them, they may attempt to lure you back with praise, remember that it is false.

Domineering Personality It is unlikely that a manipulative person will outwardly show any form of weakness. An essential part of their facade is to show conviction about their views. They seek to impress, believing they are right about everything. Almost to the point that if they realize they are wrong, they will still argue that they are right. On a one-to-one level, that invariably means that your position is always wrong. As they will chip away at your beliefs, they seek to undermine your sense of selfesteem. Once they have achieved this, then there is no holding them back.

They seek to domineer others, often speaking with a condescending tone to belittle their victims. Using ridicule is yet another tool against their target, merely because it will make themselves look better. If you ridicule them back, they will seek to turn the tables, accusing you of being oversensitive to their "joke." The kind of joke that only the teller sees the funny side.

Passive Aggressive Behavior A common trait of many hard-core manipulators is passive aggressive behavior. Because they prefer to be popular, they do not wish to be seen as doing anything wrong. Not that a manipulator would ever admit to doing anything wrong. They are experts with facial expressions that are meant to dominate and intimidate. This may include; knitting eyebrows, grinding teeth and rolling eyes. It may also include noises such as tutting and grunting sounds. It is a widespread behavior for such a character, as little anyone else has to say that they will agree upon. For most manipulators, it is their life's ambition to show people up by proving them wrong.

This can range from the aggressive look, where they seek to stare their target down. Or, it could be in response to their disagreement on something their target said. They may smirk and shake their head, turn their back, anything to show their strong disapproval. It is all a ploy to make themselves look superior and put others down.

Moody Blues What of emotional stability of the manipulator? Is it that which makes them behave the way they do? Do they even know what happiness is? The answer to that is a most definite yes, at least to the latter.

Happiness is a tool used initially to help them manipulate, a happy target is more likely to comply. In itself, this makes the manipulator happy, or at least in a sense of what they consider happiness. But their joyfulness is a perverted model of what most others believe happiness to be. Their happiness is often built on the foundations of another's misery. A misery that they have caused with their cruel manipulations. Equally though, a manipulator is prone to mood swings. Most likely to happen when things are not going to plan. One minute they are euphoric at their latest conquest. Then next they could be wholly deflated at their failure to succeed. One thing is sure for those who live with or become a target of this type of authoritarian character, they will be unhappy all the time.

Intimidation One aspect of manipulation, often used as a last resort, is intimidation and bullying. When everything else has failed, they begin to use threats to get their way. Some though may use intimidation from the onset. It may in a source of authority. For example, let's take the role of a manipulative boss. You have requested a day off. They don't want to allow you your request but have no choice, it is your right. This type of person would want their pound of flesh first. They will set goals for you to delay or cancel your request, such as moving project deadlines forward. This way they have their little victory over you.

Alternatively, such a manipulator may use the tactic of the silent treatment. Ignoring someone to the point that it becomes apparent you have displeased them. They seek to make you feel the guilty party.

Other more direct intimidating actions may include stance. Using their height or build to tower over you, or standing uncomfortably close.

Be careful as they will seek revenge for wrongdoings, they perceive done to them. Nothing will go unnoticed under their

watchful eye. Everyone is a potential target. But the weak are more likely to walk into their traps, because they are the ones who are easier to dominate. The vulnerable will have little resistance and are easier to bully and coerce. Many of these traits seem more fitting to men, but women can be cruelly manipulative too.

This is a person who will never back down in an argument. Never admit they are wrong. Never apologize for anything. A manipulator will never show respect but will expect everyone else to show them respect.

They love nothing more than to embarrass others. Playing the dumb one is common practice, just to force another person to explain themselves further. At every opportunity, the manipulator will jump in with some sarcastic remark, "hurry up, we're all waiting for your intellectual explanation," or "why has no one else ever heard of this?" Their sole aim is to make the other person look a fool, but without seeming to be the one who made it happen. Oh no, the victim did that to themselves because they are stupid.

Chapter 12. How to Spot Manipulation

Trying to figure out when somebody is taking advantage of you can be difficult. There are absolutely signs that you can watch out for. Many different great articles are surrounding the thoughts of somebody is not trying to take advantage of you. The ability to see when somebody's intentions are less than pure will keep yourself better protected and lead a happier life. It can be very frustrating when you're uncertain of someone's intentions and even worse when you find out they were simply around to take advantage of you.

People are pretty crafty, and they will use your emotions against you. Some people love to feign confusion. You may have made it very clear what your expectations are, and they simply pretend that they don't understand. If somebody you know reasonably well, it can be easy to see that they are trying to take advantage of you because you may see that they're quite smart and usually catch on to things quickly. However, if you're dealing with somebody you don't know very well you may assume that they're not very intelligent

and need a lot of direction to get something done. They're active confusion can be frustrating and leave you dealing with whatever you asked of them.

Divert Attention When people are trying to take advantage of you, they may use diversion techniques. By throwing you off a particular thought or path, they can easily change the subject and get their eyes off. Being aware and staying on track of what you were saying is essential. This goes hand-in-hand with knowing what you're going to say and spending the time to think before you speak. With clear concise thoughts you won't have to worry about people trying to divert your attention away from them.

When people try to divert attention often, they are trying to blame somebody else. This is a dangerous game and can end up pitting you against a friend, co-worker, or family member. As noted, it's essential to have your thoughts collected before entering into any serious conversation. It truly can help ensure that you do not get taken advantage of by skilled and diversion techniques.

Some people will do their very best to make you feel guilty to take advantage of you. This commonly happens with people that know you better than others. When those around you are aware that you strive to be a good person, it can be used against you. There is nothing wrong with wanting to be a good person, but it does tend to make people feel guiltier when they've done something wrong.

Everyone has moments in time where they're not the best person and that's okay. Accepting that everyone makes mistakes can help ensure that those around you cannot use guilt to control you. Sure, most of us want to make good decisions and do the right thing ourselves and those around us. Knowing that this is not always the case and we all have screw-ups is very helpful. Guilt is a common denominator and taking control over somebody or using them to your advantage.

Denial Denial is another component that people frequently used to take advantage of others. If you don't have hard evidence against somebody to stop them from simply saying no, I didn't do that. It then comes down to your word against

theirs. If somebody is vehemently denying what you are saying eventually you start to believe it. You may question the information and where you got it. This can cause distrust among those that you trust the most.

Denial is dangerous especially when you trust your sources. Hearsay is a difficult thing to prove, however, it can be very detrimental to someone's psyche. As you doubt whether your accusations are right you may also start to doubt other things in your life. This allows control to the person that is making all of the denials. They can pray on this to try and bend you to their well. Besides, once they have made you accept that their rejection is real, they might start looking for favors.

Neuro-linguistic programming skills can help in this department. Most people that are quick to deny something have some facial movements or body movements to give them away. When you start to study these techniques, it can be much simpler to figure out who is riding the denial train. When you understand that somebody is merely denying the accusations to save face or keep themselves out of trouble, it becomes easier to figure it out and understand what's going on.

Lie Liars are all around us. From the time we are little there are lies in our lives. Ones that we have told and ones that others have told us. Liars are, typically, trying to take advantage of you. Sometimes the lie that is said is relatively harmless and can be brushed off. Other times, they are significant lies that can ruin lives.

We talked a bit about lying earlier and when it comes down to it every person in the world tells a lie on occasion. When we tell a lie with good intent it doesn't make it much better than aligning with malicious intent, but it is more understandable. Sometimes, it is simply easier to tell a white lie than to hurt somebody's feelings or cause turmoil for somebody you care about.

Seduction Another way that people try to take advantage of others is with seduction. Let's face it, we all want to be accepted in love. Some people will use charm and flattery to get you on their side of the fence. They make you feel truly special but then end up merely getting what they want. They honestly, don't care about you one way or the other.

Recognizing when somebody is trying to seduce you can be challenging. If you are in a relationship and somebody is hitting on you it may be easier to blow off. Other times, when you're single and lonely, you are leaving yourself completely open to being taken advantage of. This can happen in your dating life, work life, or even in your everyday life.

Seduction seriously plays with your emotions. Your mental stability is being challenged when you allow somebody to seduce you. Taking the time to truly get to know someone before you fall for their witty comments and compliments is crucial and keeping yourself protected against being taken advantage of.

You can ward off this kind of behavior by setting clear ground rules from the beginning. It doesn't matter if you are talking with a future lover or your boss. When people understand the ground you keep, it makes them less apt to try and take advantage of you and your emotions. Those that take advantage of your feelings are the worst as it can be tough to separate your rational thinking from your emotional thinking.

When you practice NLP and start to get into the inner workings, it can keep you better protected from these emotional abusers. You will choose whether or not somebody has the ability to affect you. Not only that, you will have the ability to choose between what that affect is going to be. Having better control over yourself and your emotions will help him be better protected against those who would like to play on them.

The Art of Mindfulness A great way to add to your arsenal of maintaining control of yourself and not allowing others to take advantage or manipulate you is to practice the art of mindfulness. Mindfulness is something that we can practice every single day. There are truly some straightforward exercises that can help you become more aware of what is going on around you and inside of you. Being mindful can help keep you well protected against those who wish to do you harm or have you done their bidding.

Understandably, not everybody has a long period in a day to sit and meditate. You don't have to have a lot of time to become more mindful. It can truly only take a few minutes

per day and you'll be surprised by the results. You will notice a lot more of what is happening around you and this is, obviously, advantageous to you and your overall well-being.

One straightforward exercise that you can do pretty much throughout your day is breathing mindfully. This means that you will change your focus from whatever it is in front of you and focus on breathing in and breathing out. Notice how it feels, the sound it makes to you, and the speed at which it is happening. The more mindful you are of your breathing the more you'll focus on other things around you with continued practice.

Mindful listening is also a straightforward exercise that can help to improve your senses. When you have a few minutes, you can close your eyes and take in, literally, every noise around you. Whether you are in the office or out for a walk in the woods The Sounds will change dramatically. Home in on each one individually. Noticed what the sound is. its tone, how it makes you feel, and how it interacts with the other sounds in the room. This practice can be done for 30 seconds or even longer. Finding the time to do it should be barely an inconvenience.

Mindful observation is a great tool to have in your kit. This is the one that is going to allow you to notice the behaviors of the people around you. By sitting back and observing what is going on without participating in it is surprising how many different things you will notice. We're not only talking about observing the people around you but also the surrounding itself.

Let's say you're sitting in a board meeting and you notice that the person in the corner is a little more agitated than everyone else. By looking around the room you may notice that the air is circulating to every place except for that corner. It is likely, the person is feeling irritated because they're overheated. This may not be something that a person would notice without practicing mindful observation.

Chapter 13. Covert Emotional Manipulation

Covert emotional manipulation is used by people who want to gain power or control over you by deploying deceptive and underhanded tactics. Such people want to change the way you think and behave without realizing what they are doing. In other words, they use techniques that can alter your perceptions in such a way that you think that you are doing it out of your own free will. Covert emotional manipulation is "covert" because it works without you being consciously aware of that fact. People who are good at deploying such techniques can get you to do their bidding without your knowledge; they can hold you psychologically captive.

Covert emotional manipulation is more common than you might think. Since its subtle, people are rarely aware that it's happening to them, and in some cases, they may never even notice. Only keen outside observers may be able to tell when this form of manipulation is going on.

You might know someone who used to be fun and friendly, then she got into a relationship with someone else, and a few years down the line, she seems to have a completely different personality. If it's an old friend, you might not even recognize the person she has become. That is how powerful covert emotional manipulation can be. It can completely overhaul someone's personality without them even realizing it. The manipulator will chip away at you little by little, and you will accept minute changes that fly under the radar until the old you are replaced by a different version of you, build to be subservient to the manipulator.

Covert emotional manipulation works like a slow-moving coup. It requires you to make small progressive concessions to the person that is trying to manipulate you. In other words, you let go of tiny aspects of your identity to accommodate the manipulative person, so it never registers in your mind that there is something bigger at play.

When the manipulative person pushes you to change in small ways, you will comply because you don't want to sweat the small stuff. However, there is a domino effect that occurs as you start conceding to the manipulative person. You will be more comfortable making subsequent concessions, and your

personality will be erased and replaced in a cumulative progression.

Covert emotional manipulation occurs to some extent in all social dynamics. Look at how it plays out in romantic relationships, in friendships, and at work.

Emotional manipulation in relationships   There are many emotional manipulations in romantic relationships, and it's not always malicious. For example, women try to modify men's behavior to make them more "housebroken"; that is just normal. However, specific instances of manipulation where the person's intention is malicious, and he/she is motivated by a need to control or dominate over the other person.

Positive reinforcement is perhaps the most used covert manipulation technique in romantic relationships. Your partner can get you to do what he wants by praising you, flattering you, giving you attention, offering your gifts, and acting affectionately.

Even the seemingly nice things in relationships can turn out to be covert manipulation tools and props. For instance, your

girlfriend could use intense sex as a weapon to reinforce a certain kind of behavior in you. Similarly, men can use charm, appreciation, or gifts to reinforce certain behaviors in the women they are dating.

Some sophisticated manipulators use what psychologists call intermittent positive reinforcement to gain control over their partners. They will shower the victim with intense positive reinforcement for a certain period and then switch to just giving her regular attention and appreciation levels. After a random interval of time, he will again go back to the intense positive reinforcement. When the victim gets used to the special treatment, it's taken away, and when she gets used to standard therapy, the special treatment is brought back, and it all seems arbitrary. Now, the victim will get to a place where she becomes sort of "addicted" to the special treatment, but she has no idea how to get it, so she starts doing whatever the perpetrator wants in the hope that one of the things she does will bring back the intense positive reinforcement. In other words, she effectively becomes subservient to the perpetrator.

Negative reinforcement techniques are also used in relationships to manipulate others covertly. For example,

partners can withhold sex to compelling the other person to modify their behavior in a specific way. People also use techniques such as the silent treatment and withholding of love and affection.

Some malicious people can create a false sense of intimacy by pretending to open up to you. They could share personal stories and talk about their hopes and fears. When they do this, they create the impression that they trust you, but their intention may be to get you to feel a sense of obligation towards them.

Manipulators also use well-calculated insinuations to get you to react in a certain way at the moment to modify your behavior in the long run. People in relationships are always trying to figure out what the other person wants out of that relationship. A manipulative person can drop hints to get you to do what they want without having responsibility for your actions because they can always argue that you misinterpreted what they meant.

Dropping hints isn't always malicious (for example, if your girlfriend wants you to propose, she may leave bridal magazines out on the table). However, malicious

insinuations can be very hurtful, and they can chip away at your self-esteem. Your partner can suggest you are gaining weight, and you aren't making enough money or suggesting that your cooking skills aren't any good. People use insinuations to get away with "saying without saying," any number of hurtful things that could affect your self-esteem.

Emotional manipulations in friendships Covert emotional manipulation is quite common in friendships and casual relationships. Friendships tend to progress slower than romantic relationships, but that means that it can take a lot more time for you to figure out if your friends are manipulative. Manipulation in friendships can be confusing because even well-meaning friends can come across as malicious. That's because there is a certain social rivalry between even the closest friends, which explains the concept of "frenemies."

Manipulative friends tend to be passive-aggressive. This is where they manipulate you into doing what they want by involving mutual friends rather than directly coming to you. Passive aggression works as a manipulation technique because it denies you a chance of directly addressing whatever issue your friend is raising. So, you lose by default.

For example, if a friend wants you to do her a favor, instead of coming out and asking you, she goes to a mutual friend and suggests that she asks you on her behalf. When a mutual friend approaches you, it becomes tough for you to turn down the request because of added social pressure. When you say no, your whole social circle now perceives you as selfish.

Passive aggression can also involve the use of silent treatment to get you to comply with a request. Imagine where one of your friends talks to everyone else but you. It's going to be incredibly awkward for you, and everyone will start prying, wondering what the problem is between the two of you, and taking sides on the matter.

Friends can also covertly manipulate you by using subtle insults. They can give you back-handed compliments that have hidden meanings. What they meant by the compliment, you will realize that it's an insult in disguise, which will bruise your self-esteem and possibly modify your behavior.

Some friends can manipulate you by going on a "power trip" and controlling your social interactions. For example, there are those friends who insist that every time you hang out, it should be in their apartment or at a social venue of their choosing. Such friends often intend to dominate your friendship, so they are keen to always have the "home ground advantage" over you. They'll try to push you out of your comfort zone just so that you can reveal your weaknesses, and you can then become more emotionally reliant on them.

Manipulative friends tend to excessively capitalize on your friendship, and to a disproportionate degree. They will ask you for lots of favors with no regard for your time or your effort. They are the friends who will leverage your friendship every time they need something but then make excuses when it's their turn to reciprocate.

Emotional manipulation at work There are some reasons why your colleague may want to manipulate you. It could be you are on the same career path, so he wants to make you look bad. It could be that he is lazy, and he wants to stick you with his responsibilities. It could also be that he is a sadist, and he wants to see you suffer.

One-way people at work exert their dominance over others is by stressing them out and then, almost immediately, relieving the stress. Say, for example, you make a minor error on a report, and your boss calls you into his office. He makes a big fuss and threatens to fire you, but then towards the end, he switches gears and reassures you that your job is secure as long as you do what he wants. That kind of manipulation works on people because it makes them afraid and gives them a sense of obligation at the same time.

Some colleagues can manipulate you by doing you small favors and then reminding you of those favors every time they want something from you. For instance, if you made an error at work and a colleague covered for you, he may hold it over your head for months or even years to come, and he is going to guilt you into feeling indebted to him.

Colleagues can also manipulate you by leaving you out of the loop when passing across important information. The intention here is to get you to mess up so that they can better stand with the boss or with other colleagues. When you discover that someone is leaving you out of the loop at work and you confront them, they could feign innocence and

pretend that it was a genuine mistake on their part, or they could find a way to turn it around and blame you.

People with dark personality traits tend to be hypercompetitive at work, and they won't hesitate to use underhanded means to pull one over you. Most colleagues turn out to be good friends, but you should be careful with colleagues that are overly eager to befriend you. It could be that they want to learn more about you so that they can figure out your strengths and weaknesses and find ways to use them against you. Narcissists, Machiavellians, and psychopaths are very good at scheming at work, so don't let them catch you off guard.

Chapter 14.Laws of Manipulation

Manipulators respond to one, two, or more tactics to reach their aims, always at someone else's expense. While the strategies may vary from manipulator to manipulator, there are 13 manipulative laws each manipulator uses at one time or another:

Law #1 - Hide Your Intentions. Lying may be the oldest and most effective manipulative form around. Manipulators often respond to this strategy when trying to avoid responsibility or twist the truth. Some manipulators also admit to lies where there is no particular justification to do so, only living on the joy of causing confusion or knowing that they play with someone else's emotions. A talented manipulator knows how to operate so subtly on this angle that you don't even realize the lie they are spinning until it's too late. There may be various reasons why a manipulator

needs to resort to telling lies. It could be another to take advantage of. To hide their true intentions, so that you do not know what they are up to. Or maybe even to level out the playing field so they can stay a point ahead of you.

Law #2 - Attention Seeking. A little excitement in existence makes things exciting but chaos occurs all too much for a manipulator. Why? For what? And they set it up intentionally. Manipulators want to be the center of focus for validating themselves and offering their egos the boost of trust they feel they deserve. A friend at work may have recourse to generating friction among colleague A and colleague B by sharing tales about each other. This guarantees that while colleagues A or B are at odds with one another, they transform to a manipulator for "comfort," making the manipulator look special afterward. One person may continuously pick a conflict in a partnership to ensure that the other's energy is consistently centered on them and attempting to fix an issue that does not exist.

Law #3 - Behaving Emotionally. Manipulators may be individuals who are incredibly emotional, prone to sensational, and even hysterical rantings whenever they want stuff accomplished their way. Overly dramatic, rude, offensive, over-the-top, a manipulator can revert to irrational actions even at the smallest provocation, which is unacceptable in a social environment. A pair fighting aggressively in the cafeteria when one spouse is acting unreasonably because things are not handled their way resort to this action, thinking that their spouse will feel humiliated sufficiently to cede to their requests allows this an incredibly successful coercion tactic when employed correctly.

Law #4 - Playing Victim. Everybody always feels bad. They appear to have the world's most challenging luck. Any issue you might have, they search a way of making you feel bad for even thinking about that by finding out how "10 times worse" their problem is than yours. Now and again we all profit from a bit of bad luck; however, the

manipulator has learned to use that unfortunate streak skillfully to raise their own "victim" status and to place themselves above all others. A buddy who is continually bringing up all the harmful elements of his life when ignoring the problems will resort to this cynical technique to get the publicity they seek. Tell them you've got a rough day since you've had a flat tire on the drive to work the next morning and they'll remind you how fortunate you could still have a vehicle to worry about because they're trying to suffer the public transit difficulties. Manipulators use this emotionally exhausting technique to receive support from people, that is another means of getting publicity and ensuring that all is centered on them.

Law #5 - Taking Credit Where It's Not Due. Manipulators don't hesitate to get you to do all of the legwork, and afterward, swoop in at the last moment to take credit as they did the lion's job. A common tactic that is often used in a skilled setting, generally in group or team-work projects. Such crafty manipulators are fluttering around delegating tasks,

apparently "busy" when they don't do much at all. However, when it comes to claiming credit, they have no problem brushing you back and demanding credit for the innovations and the effort you've put into it.

Law #6 - Depend on Me. Manipulators want you, in your life, to feel like you need them. That you just can't live without them. They are the "popular" ones in a social setting to which everybody seems to flock, making you anxious to want to become a part of that community. They might be the partner in a relationship that keeps reminding you "what you would do without me" or "how you would survive without me." They do you favor and assist you out at a moment when you need it the most, going to make you feel deeply in debt to them so that at a later date they can come as well as cash in on those favors.

Law #7 - Selective Honesty. Have you ever felt so enchanted by how a generous person you know could unexpectedly turn around and stab you back? Or felt so wrong-footed when you recognized you only knew half of what was going on?

That's because the person who was feeding you with data was a manipulator. You feel stabbed in the back or wrong-footed because they only fed you information that they wanted you to know while intentionally withholding the rest. Selective honesty, a controlling manipulative tactic that can be used to charm an unsuspecting "victim".

Law #8 - Pretending to Be A "Friend". Don't be deceived by the exceedingly pleasant person you merely met at the office on your first day. They might claim to be your buddy while collecting information regarding you to use to everyone's advantage later. While some individuals may be genuinely friendly, if this individual is a little too pleasant, start raising the red flag by posing very specific or inquiring questions, especially if you've just met them. Inside a professional environment, this technique is popular and if your gut tells you something wrong, it's off.

Law #9 - Non-Committal. Do you know whoever has a hard time willing to commit to anything in your life? Even after you told them how essential it is and just now you could use their support? The non-committal person is not your mate, they are a manipulator. They find delight in withholding their authorization or support if it means they have a chance to give themselves the advantage to control the situation to their advantage. They look out for themselves and significantly deter from contributing to something if it involves taking liability. Being non-committal is a tactic of manipulation which is often used in romantic relations. When a romantic partner is non-committal, it helps keep the other on their feet and keeps them coming back for even more, thus giving the upper hand to the manipulator. The longer they withhold their dedication, the more you will be willing to bend backward, just to get their approval.

Law #10 - Playing Dumb. Is that friend you do not know what's going on? Or will they feign ignorance to prevent shouldering additional workload? Playing stupid is a deceitful tactic that is often neglected, but if people pay attention, you will find that evident in a lot of talented settings. If you were a community project leader at work, should you delegate the extra duty to the one member of the team who "wasn't as confident about anything?" Or assign that additional responsibility to someone else? The worker who was "playing stupid" tries to get away with just doing far less but receiving the same quantity of recognition in the group as everyone else. When a community of friends is in disagreement, could one person who "doesn't realize what's going on" say the truth? Or may they be feigning ignorance, realizing full well that they were solely liable for causing the conflict? In a loving relationship, can your spouse, who "doesn't know what you're talking about," tell the truth about a problem when you interrogate them? Or could they be "acting foolish" to stop getting swept up in a lie? The "innocent party" may not have been so innocent at times, after all.

Law #11 - Pointing the Finger at Others. In the first place, a manipulator would always strive to maintain their hands clean, never take accountability, and in the second place by still attempting to point a finger at somebody else because they get off brit-free when a problem arises. Significantly when that issue might endanger their credibility and reveal them besides who they are. You could be trying to deal with a manipulator if you know someone in your relatives, mates, or even with other coworkers who always criticize everything and anyone other than themselves. Keep an eye out for anyone who's behavior pattern always involves making someone the scapegoat.

Law #12 - Telling You What You Want to Hear. When you're flattered, it's impossible not to think good and you're more willing to like the person who

does all the fashionable more than the others. If one person constantly asks you all the stuff you want to learn in your life, wouldn't you be more likely to pursue them or invest more time around them? It's impossible not to think good about such people but tell you all the stuff you would like to listen to is not certainly a better friend's sign. They might be buttering you so that at a later date they can money in on a big favor that you will be "guilty" to help them with "because they were so nice to you."

Law #13 - Controlling Your Decisions. A classic setting is within a loving relationship when there is manipulation in regulating another's decision. While it is completely normal for your partner to base or start changing your decisions, is it because there is a genuine desire within you to make them happy? Or do you do it because you don't want them to risk getting angry? There is a very fine line in one relationship between what constitutes deception. If you find yourself with friends canceling schemes far too often because your partner conveys their

disappointment or makes you feel bad, manipulation in the play. It's a subtle type of coercion if you keep from wearing clothing that your partner criticizes or having a haircut after your partner said "they don't like short hair" They are manipulating the choices without actually making it clear they are. It could start casually enough with a comment or two, with something so negligible like conveying how the clothes you wear don't look better on you. The kind of dress you wear should be something else especially if you find that their things have turned into nothing more than decisions that don't make you happy because they are dictated by somebody who claims to love you.

Chapter 15. Dark Persuasion Method

Persuasion is an interesting topic. There are lots of persuasions that are considered just fine in society. They are acceptable, and even some people hold jobs where they will spend a lot of time trying to persuade others. Any attempt by one person to influence someone else to do some action can be persuasion. A salesperson at a car dealership is using persuasion because they try to persuade someone to purchase a new vehicle. This isn't seen as something sinister or bad. The difference here is that this persuasion and other similar examples of persuasion benefit both parties. The car dealer makes a sale and some money, and the "victim" is going to get a new vehicle.

There are a lot of legitimate types of persuasion that aren't considered part of dark psychology. The car dealer above is an example. If a negotiator uses their skills to persuade a terrorist to let their hostage go, this is a good form of persuasion. If you convince someone to come along to an event that they will enjoy, then this is a good form of

persuasion. This type of persuasion is seen as positive persuasion. But then, what would count as dark persuasion?

Understanding Dark Persuasion The first difference you will notice between positive and dark persuasion is the motive behind it. Positive persuasion is used in order to encourage someone to complete an action that isn't going to cause them any harm. In some cases, such as with the negotiator saving a hostage, this persuasion can be used to help save lives.

But with dark persuasion, there isn't really any form of moral motive. The motive is usually amoral, and often immoral. If positive persuasion is understood as a way to help people help themselves, then dark persuasion is more of the process of making people act against their own self-interest. Sometimes, people are going to do these actions begrudgingly, knowing that they are probably not making the right choice, but they do it because they are eager to stop the incessant persuasion efforts. In other cases, the best dark persuader is going to make their victim think that they acted wisely, but the victim is actually doing the opposite in that case.

So, what are the motivations for someone who is a dark persuader? This is going to depend on the situation and the individual who is doing the persuading. Some people like to persuade their victims in order to serve their own selfinterests. Others are going to act through with the intention just to cause some harm to the other person. In some cases, the persuader is not going to really benefit from darkly persuading their victim, but they do so because they want to inflict pain on the other person. And still, others enjoy the control that this kind of persuasion gives to them.

You will also find that the outcome you get from dark persuasion is going to differ from what happens with positive persuasion. With positive persuasion, you are going to get one of three scenarios including the following:

• The benefit goes to the person who is being persuaded.

• There is a win/win benefit for the persuaded and the persuader.

• There is a mutual benefit for the person who is persuaded and a third party.

All of these outcomes are good because they will involve a positive result for the person who is being persuaded. Sometimes, there will be others who benefit from these actions. But out of all three situations, the persuaded party is always going to benefit.

With dark persuasion, the outcome is going to be very different. The persuader is the one who will always benefit when they exercise their need for influence or control. The one who is being persuaded often goes against what is in their self-interest when they listen, and they are not going to benefit from all this dark persuasion.

In addition, the most skilled dark persuaders are not only able to cause some harm to their victims while also benefiting themselves, but they could also end up harming others in the process.

Unmasking the Dark Persuader At this point, you may be curious about who is using these dark methods of persuasion. Are there actually people out there who are interested in using this kind of persuasion and using it against others to cause harm?

The main characteristics of a dark persuader are either an indifference toward or an inability to care about how persuasion is going to impact others. Such people who use this kind of persuasion are going to be often narcissistic and will see their own needs as more important than the needs of others. They may even be sociopathic and unable to grasp the idea of someone else's emotions.

Many times, this kind of dark persuasion is going to show up in a relationship. Often one but sometimes both partners are going to be inclined towards trying to use dark persuasion on each other. If these attempts are persistent and endure, then this type of relationship is going to be classified as psychologically abusive, and that is not healthy for the victim in that relationship. Often, they will not realize that there is something going on or that they are darkly persuaded until it is too late, and they are stuck there.

There are many examples of using this kind of dark persuasion in a relationship. If one partner stops the other partner from taking a new job opportunity or doesn't allow them to go out with friends, then this could be an example of dark persuasion. The dark persuader will work to convince the victim that they are acting in a way that is best for the

relationship. In reality, the victim is going through a process that harms them and the relationship.

Dark Persuasion Techniques to Be on the Lookout For After taking a look at the different types of persuasion and what they all mean, you may be able to see why dark persuasion such a bad thing is and can be harmful to the victim. Being able to recognize the different techniques that the manipulator may use can make it easier to understand when it is being used on you.

So, how exactly is a dark persuader able to use this idea in order to carry out their wishes? There are a few different types of tactics that a dark manipulator is going to use, but some of the most common options include:

The Long Con The first method that we are going to look at is the Long Con. This method is kind of slow and drawn out, but it can be really effective because it takes so long and is hard to recognize or even pinpoint when something went wrong. One of the main reasons that some people have the ability to

resist persuasion is because they feel that they are being pressured by the other person, and this can make them back off. If they feel that there is a lack of rapport or trust with the person who is trying to persuade them, they will steer clear as well. The Long Con is so effective because they are able to overcome these main problems and give the persuader exactly what they want.

The Long Con is going to involve the dark persuader to take their time, working to earn the trust of their victim. They are going to take some time to befriend the victim and make sure that their victim trusts and likes them. This is going to be achieved by the persuader with artificial rapport building, which sometimes seems excessive, and other techniques that will help to increase the comfort levels between the persuader and their victim.

As soon as the persuader sees that the victim is properly readied psychologically, the persuader is going to begin their attempts. They may start out with some insincere positive persuasion. The persuader is going to lead their victim into making a choice or doing some action that will actually benefit the persuader. This is going to serve the persuader in two ways. First, the victim starts to become used to

persuasion by that persuader. The second is that the victim is going to start making that mental association between a positive outcome and the persuasion.

The Long Con is going to take a long period of time to complete because the persuader doesn't want to make it too obvious what they are doing. An example of this is a victim who is a recently widowed lady who is vulnerable because of her age and from their bereavement. After her loss, a man starts to befriend her. This man may be someone she knows from church or even a relative. He starts to spend more time with her, showing immense kindness and patience, and it doesn't take too long for her guard to drop when he comes around.

Then this man starts to carry out some smaller acts of positive persuasion that we talked about before. He may advise her of a better bank account to use or a better way to reduce any monthly bills. The victim is going to appreciate these efforts and the fact that the man is trying to help her, and she takes the advice.

Over some time, the man then tries to use some dark persuasion. He may try to persuade her to let him invest some of her money. She obliges because of the positive persuasion that was used in the past. Of course, the man is going to work to take everything he can get from her. If the manipulator is skilled enough, she may feel that he actually tried to help her, but the money is lost because he just ran into some bad luck with the investment. This is how far dark persuasion can go.

Gradualism Often when we hear about acts of dark persuasion, it seems impossible and unbelievable. What they fail to realize is that this dark persuasion isn't ever going to be a big or a sudden request that comes out of nowhere. Dark persuasion is more like a staircase. The dark persuader is never going to ask the victim to do something big and dramatic the first time they meet. Instead, they will have the victim take one step at a time.

When the manipulator has the target only go one step at a time, the whole process seems like less of a big deal. Before the victim knows it, they have already gone a long way down, and the persuader isn't likely to let them leave or come back up again.

Let's take an example of how this process is going to look in real life. Let's say that there is a criminal who wanted to make it so that someone else committed the crimes for them. Gang bosses, cult leaders, and even Charles Manson did this exact same thing.

This criminal wouldn't dream of beginning the process by asking their victim to murder for them.

Chapter 16.Neuro Linguistic Programming

What is NLP

Neuro-Linguistic Programming has to do with the study of thoughts (neuro) and language (linguistic) in a systemic way and the scripts that run the life of an individual (programming).

It deals with the understanding and the development of the mind and the entire understanding of the language of the mind in relation to the way it is designed to function and the ways in which it is molded by the personal experiences of an individual. It is simply a study of a person's subjective reality.

A proper understanding of the language of the mind influences every aspect of a person's life from his relationship with others to his communication skills with friends and clients to the general outcome of a person's life. It is a holistic study that puts the spirit, body, past and present of an individual into consideration.

As Homo sapiens who are gifted with the ability to think, it is presumed that our most important function is the thought or

the thinking function. NLP, however, brings one to the understanding of the fact that no thought process exists in a vacuum, as they are a product of a person's perspective. It has a presupposition of perception as reality and it holds that the things, we think are colored by the way we think.

For different individuals there are different ways of thinking and interpreting reality. What NLP does is assist in the understanding of these various representational systems to help each person narrow down his own system. It helps in the understanding of the three different types of thinking patterns which are:

- Visual - deals with both pictures and visual metaphors.

- Auditory - sound (hearing).

- Kinesthetic - deals with the five senses, as well as gut feelings.

In NLP, a person is thought to take absolute control of his mind and ultimately his life. Unlike what is obtainable in psychoanalysis, which places its focus on "why," NLP presents a more practical approach with its focus on the "how."

How NLP Works

If you are just coming across this topic for the first time, NLP may appear or seem like magic or hypnosis. When a person is undergoing therapy, this topic digs deep into the unconscious mind of the patient and filters through different layers of beliefs and the person's approach or perception of life to deduce the early childhood experiences that are responsible for a behavioral pattern.

In NLP, it is believed that everyone has the resources that are needed for positive changes in their own lives. The technique adopted here is meant to help in facilitating these changes.

Usually, when NLP is taught, it is done in a pyramidal structure. However, the most advanced techniques are left for those multi-thousand-dollar seminars. An attempt to explain this complicated subject is to state that the NLPer (as those who use NLP will often call themselves) is always paying keen attention to the person they are working on/with.

Usually, there is a large majority of NLPers that are therapists and they are very likely to be well-meaning people. They achieve their aims by paying attention to those subtle cues like the movement of the eyes, flushing of the skin, dilation of the pupil and subtle nervous tics. It is easy for an NLP user to determine the following quickly:

• The side of the brain that the person uses predominantly.

• The sense (smell, sight, etc.) that is more dominant in a person's brain.

• The way the person's brain stores and makes use of information (the NLPer can deduce all this from the person's eye movement).

• When they are telling a lie or concocting information.

When the NLP user has successfully gathered all this information, they begin to mimic the client in a slow and subtle manner by not only taking on their body language, but also by imitating their speech and mannerisms, so that they begin to talk with the language patterns that are aimed at targeting the primary senses of the client. They will typically fake the social cues that will easily make someone let their guard down so that they become very open and suggestible.

For example, when a person's sense of sight is their most dominant sense, the NLPer will use a language that is very laden with visual metaphors to speak with them. They will say things like: "do you see what I am talking about?" or "why not look at it this way?" For a person that has a more dominant sense of hearing, he will be approached with an auditory language like: "listen to me" or "I can hear where you're coming from."

To create a rapport, the NLPer mirrors the body language and the linguistic patterns of the other person. This rapport is a mental and physiological state which a human being gets into when they lose guard of their social senses. It is done when they begin to feel like the other person who they are conversing with is just like them.

Once the NLPer have achieved this rapport, they will take charge of the interaction by leading it in a mild and subtle manner. Thanks to the fact that they have already mirrored the other person, they will now begin to make some subtle changes in order to gain a certain influence on the behavior of the person. This is also combined with some similar subtle language patterns which lead to questions and a whole phase of some other techniques.

At this point, the NLPer will be able to tweak and twist the person to whichever direction they so desire. This only happens if the other person can't deduce that there is something going on because they assume everything that is occurring is happening organically or that they have given consent to everything.

What this means is that it is quite hard to make use of NLP to get other people to act out of character, but it can be used to get a person to give responses within their normal range of character. This may come in the form of getting them to donate to a charitable cause, or finally making the decision they had been putting off or getting them to go home with you for the night if they had considered it at some previous point.

At this point, what the NLP user seeks to do may be to either elicit or anchor. When they are eliciting, they make use of both leading and language to get the person to an emotional state of say, sadness. Once they can elicit this state, they can then lead it on with a physical cue by touching the other person's shoulder for example.

According to theory, whenever the NLP user touches the person's shoulder in the same manner, the same emotional state will resurface if they do it again. However, this is only made possible by the successful conditioning of the other person.

When undergoing NLP therapy, it is very possible for the therapist to adopt a content-free approach, which means the therapist can work effectively without taking a critical look at the problem or without even knowing about the problem at all. This means that there is room for privacy for the client as

the therapist does not really need to be told about whichever event took place or whatever issue happened in the past.

Also, prior to the commencement of the therapy, there is an agreement which ensures that the therapist cannot disclose any information; hence the interaction between the therapist and the client remains confidential.

In NLP, there is the belief in the need for the perfection of the nature of human creation, so every client is encouraged to recognize the sensitivity of the senses and make use of them in responding to specific problems. As a matter of fact, NLP also holds the belief that it is possible for the mind to find cures to diseases and sicknesses.

The techniques employed by NLP have to do with a noninvasive, medicine-free therapy that enables the client to find out new ways of handling emotional issues such as low self-esteem, lack of confidence, anxiety and destructive relationship patterns. It is also a successful tool in effective bereavement counseling.

With its roots in the field of behavioral science, which was developed by Skinner, Pavlov and Thorndike, NLP makes use of the combination physiology and the unconscious mind to bring about change in the thought process and ultimately the behavior of a person.

The Importance of NLP Neuro-Linguistic Programming is not only necessary for the understanding of a person's being, but it also helps in the understanding of the way an individual is. It helps a person to get deep into the root cause of the problem, as well as the foundation of their being.

Here are some other reasons why NLP is important:

- It helps people take responsibility for the things that they feel they may not be able to control. With the help of NLP, it is possible for a person to change the way they react to events of the past and have a certain level of control over their future.

- It is very important for people to be aware of the body language of the members of their inner circle, as well as those who they seek to do business with. With NLP, it is possible to make use of language with both control and purpose, and with this it is possible to have control over your life.

Remember, you cannot expect to make the same mistakes using the same mindset and hope to get different results. During an NLP session, the focus is placed entirely on the client as they are made the subject. This helps a lot because at the point where a person can deal with his or herself as a

person, they gain more clarity into his or her dealings with other people.

- It helps to improve finance, sales performance, marriage, health issues, parenting, customer service and every other aspect and phase of life. This is because it helps in the holistic improvement of an individual and when a person is whole, his interactions and relationship with himself and other people become whole as well.

- It assists in targeting your beliefs, thoughts and values and helps with the targeting of a person's brain functions, as well as developing certain behaviors. It also shapes the way these behaviors metamorphoses into habits and how the habits change to actions which in turn comes as results.

NLP is applicable in different vocations and professions. This is a tool that is very important in the mastery of sales, personal development experts and self-help, teaching, communication, parenting and other facets of life.

Chapter 17.Making NLP effective

When it comes to managing people effectively, it's important that you first understand the non-verbal cues they provide, to be able to apply your skills toward influencing them. This is an important principle in applying the NLP technique. Following are a few NLP techniques that can allow you to influence people's perception and thinking:

Deciphering Eye Movements

It is essential to understand the meaning of eye movements because each eye movement tells its tale. For instance, when searching for the right word, or trying to remember a name, you automatically move your eyes in a certain way (most likely, squinting). Rolling the eyes signals contempt, or exasperation.

Winking indicates flirtation, or a joke.

Widening the eyes signals surprise, or shock; even extreme excitement. Eye movements are also implicated in other facial expressions.

The eyes can reveal much more about people's mental and emotional status, all on their own.

Once you understand what other people's thought processes are, you can accurately follow a course of action or dialogue which acknowledges the unspoken response, as signaled by the eyes. And as you may know, eye movements complement other communication forms such as hand movements, speech, and facial expressions.

Dilation of the pupils, breathing, angle of the body, and the hands' position – all these are complementary to the spoken message. Still, eye movement is very important in communication, because every movement is influenced by particular senses and the different parts of the brain.

Here is how you can generally interpret eye movement:

Visual Responsiveness

Eyes upward, then towards the right:

> Whenever a person tilts eyes upward and then to the right, it means that the person is formulating a mental picture.

Eyes upward, then towards the left:

Whenever a person tilts eyes upward, followed by an eye movement to the left, it means the person is recalling a certain image.

Eyes looking straight ahead:

Whenever someone focuses directly in front of them, as though looking at a point in the distance, this indicates that they are not focused on anything in particular. That is the look often referred to as 'glazed'.

Auditory Responsiveness

Eyes looking towards the right:

When a person's eyes shift straight towards the right, it means the person is constructing a sound.

Eyes looking towards the left:

When a person's eyes shift straight towards the left, it indicates that the person is recalling a sound.

Audio-digital responsiveness

Eyes looking downward, then switching to the left:

When someone drops their eyes and then proceeds to turn their eyes to the left, this signals that the person is engaged in internal dialogue.

Eyes looking right down then left to right:

When a person looks downward and then proceeds to turn their eyes to the left and then, to the right in consecutive movements, it means the person is engaged in negative selftalk.

Kinesthetic Responsiveness

Here, the person looks directly down, only to turn the eyes to the right. That is an indication that the person is evaluating emotional status. This further indicates that the person is not at ease.

Verbal Responses

Rhythmic Speech The idea here is not to be poetic as you speak, but to speak regularly. The recommended pace of speaking is equated to the heartbeat, say, between 45 and 72 beats per minute. At that pace, you are likely to sustain the listener's attention and establish greater receptivity to what you're saying. While normal conversational speed averages about 140 words per minute, slowing down a little and taking time to pause is highly effective to sustain people's attention. Your regular cadence should be punctuated by fluctuations in tone and emphasis not to sound monotonous.

Repeating Key Words When you are trying to influence someone, there are key words or phrases that carry additional weight as far as your message is concerned. This speaking method is a way of embedding the message in the listener and subtly suggesting that your message is valid and worthy of reception. Repeating key words also suggests commitment, conviction and mastery of the subject matter.

Using Strongly Suggestive Language Use a supportive and positive language of what you are saying, using a selection set of strong, descriptive words or phrases. As you do this, you should observe the person you are speaking to closely, in a manner that makes them feel as

though you are seeing right through them and aware of what they are thinking. Don't be invasive about this, or aggressive.

Merely suggest that you have a keen appreciation of what makes people tick by way of your gaze. This places you in a dominant position, especially when accompanied by dominant body language, like "steepling". It helps to use suitable, complementary body language as you speak, to underscore the message subtly.

Touching the Person Lightly, As You Speak Touching the person as you speak to them draws their attention to you in a relaxed and familiar way. By employing this technique, you're preparing the listener to absorb what you are saying to them and programming attentiveness. Those engaging in inter-gender conversations in the workplace should take great care with this technique, as it can lead to misunderstandings.

Using A Mixture Of "Hot" And "Vague" Words

"Hot" words are those that tend to provoke specific sensations in the listener. When you use them to influence someone's thinking, it is advisable to use them in a suitable pattern. Examples of phrases containing hot words are: feel free; see this; because; hear this. The effect of employing these words and phrases is that you're directing influencing the listener's state of mind, including how they feel, imagine, and perceive. You're also appealing to the sense most prevalent in the listener's conscious style (as observed through the movement of their eyes).

For example, the phrase "hear this" will appeal to those who indicate a tendency to respond most actively to auditory stimuli.

Using the Interspersal Technique The interspersal technique is the practice of stating one thing while hoping to impress something entirely different on the listener. For example, you could make a positive statement like:

John is very generous, but some people take advantage of him and treat him as gullible.

When someone hears this statement, the likely assumption is that you want people to appreciate John's generosity. That is likely to be the message heard and yet, the subtext is that while John is generous, he is also considered gullible and thus, at a disadvantage in life, when it comes to other people. Your hidden agenda may be to influence the listener to think of John as gullible, which calls into question his judgment. So, emphasize the words "but" and "gullible". The word "but" serves to transition the perceived compliment to John to an implicit slight.

The techniques just described form strategies in the service of influencing people. They're not intended to force a viewpoint, or to control people's behavior for nefarious ends. These techniques are intended to modify undesirable behaviors, resulting in workplace difficulties, including the failure of staff to work well together, or to complete team projects. They're also extremely helpful in the context of relationships with young people and children, whether at home, or in a learning environment.

Techniques of subtle manipulative effect like those described, though capable of influencing people and their behavior, don't amount to anything even approaching

coercion. The person being spoken to chooses all responses and is merely influenced, or steered toward those responses.

Chapter 18.How to use NLP

Now that you are aware of what NLP is and why it is so important to include in your life, you can start to get some ideas of how you can practically apply this to everything that you do. There are many different methods, and the theories of persuasion are always going to be evolving. If you can start to include some of these methods in your life, however, you will be able to see the things that you are being persuaded of and how you can better protect against this.

The first method of NLP is to understand someone else's neuro-linguistic programming. Start first by identifying their tone of voice and the way that they speak. Are they someone who is outgoing and not afraid to share the things on their mind? Are they a person who is going to be a little quieter and someone who isn't going to state as much as someone else might? When you discover how they are able to communicate, then you will be able to match your tone with that. If they are a shy person, you don't want to attack them by being a very loud and outgoing person. This mismatch can

cause the other person to end up shutting off and keeping themselves protected because they are fearful of you and this interaction. After you have discovered this, then look at their body movements. You can actually start to mimic some of this if you want to be more persuasive. If they are sitting relaxed on the couch and lean back, you know that you can start to become a little more relaxed as well. This will create a friendly and familiar vibe in order to keep both of you comfortable. Don't be too obvious with this. If you make all the same movements that they do and only try to mimic them completely, it will come off as fake and phony and that will turn the other person off more than anything else we discuss. After this, see what you might be able to pick up from their background. Are they someone that has frequently been taught to think a certain way? Do they seem as though they come from a more open environment? This can help you identify their willingness to change and the ways in which you might have to try a little harder to get them to be on your side while you are attempting to be persuasive. Always remember to go through the acronym of NLP to try and determine what a person is really trying to say and the things that they are all about.

Next, start to try and speak in a way that is natural to their rhythm. This can be done first by noticing your heartbeat. You can put your hand on your chest or fingers on your wrist in a subtle way to determine what your heartbeat might be. Once you have found this frequency, you might start to tap your foot along with this beat. Then, start to match your breathing as well.

What you are doing is creating a pitch or frequency that will be carried throughout the room. The other person might end up following this kind of pitch and frequency, making it easier for the both of you to match up. It will be a natural way to get the two of you in tune. Then, as you are talking, try to match the rhythm of how you are sharing your words with the frequency that you had created. By doing this, you might end up making your message much more consumable by the other person. It will allow your messages to flow freely and naturally into them, and they won't be as aware of the way that you have managed to convince them. If you are listening to music and in a place where you are doing this, then you can start to match your words with the beat of the music as well.

As you are talking, it will also help if you use specific symbolic words. The more that you state this word, the easier

that it might be to end up convincing the person that they should follow through with what you are trying to persuade them of. For example, let's imagine that you are trying to convince your partner that you should buy a beach home. You have done your research on them and know that they are they the type of person that cares about relaxing more than anything. Since this can be your basis of persuasion, you will want to use words like relaxing as often as possible. You can use this word and other synonyms, such as peaceful, calm, comfortable, and so on. The more that you talk, the more you would want to emphasize these points. You can talk through the amount of money and commitment it would bring about more frequently, and instead, focus just on saying things such as comfy, cozy, relaxing, peaceful, and quiet, as often as possible

The final way we are going to discuss that you can use NLP is the anchorage method. If you were on a boat and you needed to dock it and keep it in a specific spot, you drop an anchor. If you are talking to someone and you want them on board with what you're saying, then you might anchor them so that they are going to stay in this same spot in their thought processes. An anchor will be a physical symbol that will help

keep that person in the moment. It might be something as simple as touching their shoulder gently, or it could be an actually physical object that you keep in the room. Back to the example of buying a beach house, you might anchor the person by keeping a candle that is specifically beach scented in order to help keep them focused on the things that you want to persuade them of.

How to Protect Against NLP Now that you understand just how easy it is to get started with NLP tactics, you need to ensure that you are prepared to protect yourself against it. There are always going to be people out there who might be a little more skilled than you, with more experience in the subject, making it easier to have complete control over you and the things that you decide. Remember not to be fearful or angry with them right away if you catch them using NLP methods. They might simply be like you and want to be more aware of ways that they can persuade others!

Start by ensuring that no one touches you. If you're having a conversation with your lover, of course, they might put a hand on your shoulder or hold your hand, so don't look so

deep into that. However, if you show up to a business meeting happy and excited and the other person puts their hand on your shoulder right away, this is an instant signal that they might be trying to control you from the start. It is a method of anchoring. They notice that you are in a good mood, so they might anchor you in that moment by touching you. Then, as you are leaving the business meeting, you are a little bit more tired and not as excited about going through the deal. The person touches your shoulder in the exact same way, and you can pick up on this and notice that it might be an attempt at trying to get you back into that same good mood that you started the meeting with.

After this, be cautious when you notice that someone is really going out of their way to try and mimic your body language. Of course, those who are nervous especially will be a little more likely to try and match the way that you are sitting. However, if you notice that it seems to be going above and beyond and just feels extra overall, then this might be a sign that they are trying to control you. If you believe that they are intentionally matching your body language, start to change the way that you are sitting and moving yourself. Alternate your shoulders, switch things up, and make unnatural

movements. If they keep doing the same thing, then it might be a sign that they are using NLP against you.

Make sure that you really pay attention to everything that they say. There are a few different things that they might include in their speech that could potentially go unnoticed by you. The first one is that they might be attempting to slip in words using gibberish that you don't notice. Maybe the two of you are laughing a bit, so they decide to throw some words in there that you don't hear. Later on, they can't say that they never said that, you just didn't notice. Don't let any words go unnoticed.

Be cautious of the way that they might be too vague as well. There are some words that could really go either way, and they will use these vague words to try and convince you of something by making it form in your brain in your own terms. When vague language is used, it gives you the chance to put yourself in that image and create your own ideas, making you more likely to buy into something. Have you ever noticed that a lot of the main characters of different types of TV shows look the same? This is often because basic actors are hired in order to make it easier for other people to put themselves in that situation. Think of the most popular dating shows. They will usually cast someone that looks rather similar to other people in an attempt to make it easier for viewers to put themselves in that person's shoes and envision their life through this surrogate TV personality. When basic and vague language are learned, then this will give the person that might be being persuaded a chance to really put themselves in this image. Think of any presidential slogan that you've ever seen. Words such as "hope," "change," "together," and so on are all frequently used. This is something vague that we all have or could hope to have. People will be more easily convinced to follow along with these ideas because they can really see themselves at the center of this kind of movement, no matter how different individual politics might be. If you notice that someone is using these very basic words with you, question them. If they say something like, "We are very hopeful," ask them, "About what?" They will often just state a "what" but never a "why." Always make them question and explain that "why," and it will be much easier for you to see if they are just being vague in an attempt to manipulate you.

Make sure that you are always keeping some time and distance between you and the person that might be trying to

use NLP against you. They might try to rush you and just generally get closer to be more personable. Even if you're certain that it's a good deal and that they are more than likely not being manipulative.

Chapter 19.Recognising and using subliminal messages

What is subliminal messages

This is a type of message or affirmation that is presented either visually or auditorily that is sent in a way that is below what is considered to be normal for human visual or auditory perception. For example, a record might be playing on repeat, but you cannot hear it with your conscious mind. However, deep in your subconscious, you are hearing it and fully registering everything that it is saying. In most cases, the messages used are meant to control you in some way or suggest that you do something.

For example, subliminal messages are commonly used in today's world to promote smoking cessation or weight loss. In general, you listen to recorded tapes with a specific message when you are sleeping. Your unconscious mind gets the message, but you never hear it as your conscious self. Either way, research shows that it can be an effective tool to change your smoking or eating behaviors. You can use a similar technique to aid in changing how people think to

make them more vulnerable to the types of persuasion that you prefer to use.

How to recognize a subliminal message subliminal message techniques

This is an effective way to control both your mind and the minds of others, but it can be a bit obvious when you do not use the techniques properly. As you read into the primary techniques, pay close attention to how you might introduce a person to them. This is important and ultimately your relationship with the person you are seeking to control will determine which of these techniques works the best.

Subliminal messages during sleep: This is one of the most common ways to use these types of messages. Most people will use them for themselves in this manner, but you can also use them with people you live with. For example, once you know your spouse is asleep, play a subliminal recording for about one hour. This is all it takes to get your message across.

Now, it is imperative that you know for sure that they are sleeping or else you could do more harm than good to your persuasion efforts. When you create your recording, use a calm and steady voice. State exactly what you want the person to do. Use no filler words. Use a maximum of 10 words and simply repeat it for the duration of an hour. Then, once the person is sleeping, play the recording at a very low volume close to their head so that their unconscious mind hears it.

Subliminal flashes: These do not take as long as they are not as risky as the above method. These are a type of visual subliminal message. You can create the flashes to say exactly what you want. What is nice about this technique is that the message flashes so quickly that the conscious mind often does not see what it says. Only the subconscious can understand and record it. you can get some control over a person's mind without them knowing what you are attempting to control.

Unless the person you want to do this with knows about subliminal psychology, you can just tell them you want to show them something you created. It is best to do this on a computer so that the screen is large enough to catch and keep their full attention during the flashes.

Mixed subliminal messages: You can insert subliminal messages into the music or audiobooks that someone listens to on a regular basis. There are programs that can do this, so you do not have to be a tech expert to take advantage of this method. Just like with the subliminal messages during sleep, you will use a calm and steady voice. You want the messages to mix into the audiobook or music without being detected. Remember the subconscious mind will pick up on it even when they cannot hear it when they are awake.

Just make sure to use these messages in something they listen to daily, or almost daily. It is important that they hear it regularly to gain the most control.

Subliminal notes: This is the easiest method, but it is also the simplest to figure out if you are not careful. You can put messages inside messages throughout your home. For example, when you are creating the grocery list, add something else you want, but do not normally shop for. This puts the thought in the person's head when they are reading the list. This is ideal for smaller things that you want to persuade someone to think or do. Keep it simple and use this method periodically. Unlike the above methods, it is not a good idea to use it every day.

Why are subliminal messages so powerful?

Subliminal messages are a very powerful part of mind control, and are an extremely important strategy to learn if you want to brainwash anyone successfully. Subliminal messages are so powerful that they actually exist all over the modern world, and most of us don't even recognize it. They can be found in advertising, movies, news, and much more. Learning to use subliminal messages will help you successfully use mind control on people in the most masterful way. You will be able to brainwash anyone into thinking and behaving in the way that you desire for them to behave, and you will be able to have any outcome you desire once you master this technique. This is next level mind control that many people take years to master, but you are going to learn to master it easily and efficiently with these steps.

Scaling Back

This technique is an incredible way to use subliminal messaging to get people to do what you want them to do. Using this strategy will enable you to get people where you want them to be, easily. The technique is virtually effortless, and is often used in sales and other similar situations. You can modify it to work for anything, though. Essentially, all you need to do is start with a large request and scale it back as you are talking. For example, let's say you want to get someone to talk to you on the phone. You could start by asking to hang out and perhaps go on a date together. As the conversation progresses, however, work your way backwards and simply ask for a phone call. Because it is not as grandiose and intense as the original request, they are more likely to say yes. After all, a phone call seems to bear much less pressure than a request to go on a date, right? Then, once you have them on the phone you can push for the date!

First Name Basis People absolutely love hearing their first names. It has a certain effect on people that is not achieved through virtually any other name in any language. Using someone's name is a sort of flattery that also validates someone's existence. People love knowing that they are recognized for the core of who they are, and they are much more likely to comply with what you are asking if you are using their first name regularly. You also want to refer them as what you want them to be for you. So, let's say you want "John" to become your friend. You could say "John, did you enjoy the game last night?" and when he says "Yeah, it was pretty good!" you could say "I agree, friend!" This associates them with being your friend, and is more likely to encourage them actually to feel as though they are your friend as well. This brings certain perks, such as trust, that are necessary to use brainwashing and mind control, too effectively.

Flattery

Many people argue that flattery will get you nowhere, but this is false. Flattery will get you everywhere if you use it right. People are attracted to those who are naturally charming and part of being charming is using flattery. If you take the time to charm those you are talking to, they are more likely to respond in your favor because you make them feel good. Something that is important to recognize with people, however, is the level of self-esteem they carry. Those who have high self-esteem will like to be flirted with heavily because you are validating their higher sense of self-esteem. Those who have low self-esteem, however, will become uncomfortable and intimidated if you flatter them too much. It causes them to feel as though they are being "buttered up" and makes them experience a conflict since they cannot relate to what you are saying. The more you practice identifying someone's sense of self-esteem, the easier it will be to gauge them and use this as an opportunity to flatter them in a way that will genuinely feel good to them and cause them to feel more inclined to respect your words and opinions.

One thing that is worth pointing out is that when you meet someone with extremely low self-esteem, you never want to go in the opposite direction and demean them.

This will make them feel bad and break the trust between you two. If their self-esteem is phenomenally low, consider skipping this step altogether to prevent yourself from creating a disconnect between yourself and the person you are talking to.

Paraphrasing

People love to be validated, and paraphrasing is a great way to validate them. When you paraphrase someone, they feel as though you are listening to them carefully and that you are validating what they are saying. This makes them feel good, and develops a great sense of connection between the two of you. This is an excellent way to create that connection and use it as an opportunity to establish a trust between you and the person you are talking to, while also finding your way into their subconscious mind so that you can speak past their conscious mind and into their subconscious. This is how you will get maximum success with getting them to do what you want!

Nod A Lot

Nodding is connected with a positive agreeance between you and the person you are talking to. Nodding frequently throughout the conversation instills a very positive feeling into the person you are talking to, and helps them feel as

though you are truly listening to them. When they see you nodding and agreeing with many parts of the conversation, they are going to feel more likely to nod and agree as well when it comes your turn to talk. This creates an overall positive situation where you can easily get them to agree with you, because the sense of "agreeance" is high in the conversation in general.

Repetition

One of the best ways that you can get through with subliminal messages is repetition. If you don't use repetition, your message is going to fall on deaf ears. The more you repeat certain words and phrases, the more the subconscious mind is going to hear it and you are going to have success with getting someone to agree with you and do what you want them to do. When you repeat something, it essentially "warms up" the mind to the idea, and helps people begin to really feel and believe it as the truth. The more you repeat it, the more they believe it and agree with it, and the more inclined they are to agree with it in the real world, too verbally. If you do not use repetition, you will never succeed in getting your messages and desires through to the person you are attempting to mind control.

Visual Subliminal Messages

Many people believe that audio messages are the only way to get subliminal messages through, but this is simply not true. In this day and age, we have access to text-based communications, and visually seeing the repetitive message can have a major impact on someone's likelihood of agreeing with you and making a positive connection with you and the message you are sharing. You can text your message to people without being overly obvious, and you can also find creative ways to share it on social media if you have them added. This will lead to them seeing the message beyond your conversations with them, which will even further warm their mind up to the idea and have them agreeing with you in no time.

Subliminal messages are a large part of brainwashing and mind control. These messages are generally thought to have little to no weight behind them, but they are intended to pack a punch and really leave a lasting impact on your listener without them even realizing it. To them, you may be innocently passing along a message, whereas to you, you are intentionally instilling this information into someone else's mind with ulterior motives of some sort. How use them to their advantage It is important to understand that subliminal messages are not always a positive thing. Just because you can use them to your advantage doesn't mean you should always be using them for your own personal motivation. In fact, it is possible to pick up on subliminal messages without even knowing it. These messages can be picked up on by the subconscious mind, which is an integral part of the human brain. The subconscious mind is often referred to as being the more animalistic part of our brain and it deals with our primal desires and instincts. It is important to be able to recognize these messages for what they are so that you can use them in your favor. Here are the ways you take advantage of subliminal messages:

1. Subliminal Messages If you are constantly speaking to someone about something, you will get on their mind and they might do what you want them to do, so use this strategy to your advantage. If the person is resistant about doing what you want them to do then say something like 'I'm not going to leave this conversation till I get my point across' or 'No one ever argued that this works' or anything like it, and they will agree with you once they see how persistent you are.

2. Use the replies you get from them as a strategy to brainwash them further and use these replies as an opportunity to agree with them and validate their concerns.

3. Use the power of subconscious mind by using subliminal messages in order to get them to do what they want and act in the way they want to act like and feel how they desire for them to feel like instead of making them feel bad or mad at you because it is just not going your way..

4. Always know what you are going to say before you say it and always make sure that it is in the linear form and not in the round about because linear language is easier for

people to understand especially when there are a lot of words involved, so make sure to use this trick too.

5. Use a lot of repetition and if you want to be more effective use it in places where they can see it like on social media or on texts, emails, letters etc.

6. When speaking to the person you want to brainwash, keep this thought process in mind: "I am going to have a conversation with this person about this topic and I will get this person agree with me about what I want them to agree for sure because they will start acting in the way that I want them to act and thinking the way I want them to think about something that I really want from them"

7. Always keep the image of the person you are trying to brainwash in your mind. You can do this by saying positive things about them and even saying things like "I will be successful in making him/her think about what I want them to think about because I am persistent, and they will trust me because I make them feel comfortable while we are talking"

8. Use the power of subliminal messages as well by repeating them in many different ways and using them to your advantage. You will not believe how effective these messages are.

9. Be more aware of what the person you want to brainwash has said. You will be surprised at how effective this strategy is.

10. Be aware of how you say things and always make sure that your language is clear and linear so it will be easy for the person to understand what you are saying and don't say anything in round about because it will make them confuse and they will have a hard time understanding these things especially if there are a lot of words involved, so make sure to use this trick as well.

Chapter 20. Who Uses Mind Control

Mind control can be as simple as a subliminal suggestion used to steer one in the direction you want rather than the order they were going autonomously. Every day, you are exposed to one form of mind control or another. Product placement on television and in movies. The music you hear in a store or even an elevator. Friends that are so convincing, you can't help but agree, or you find yourself always saying yes to them.

Re-education is a very optimal but controversial tool in mind control. The ability to re-educate another person's previous thought process or beliefs is possible but can take time. By repeating the same belief, idea, or thought to another person repeatedly, you impress upon them the change from their ideas towards your own. And this repetition leads to immersion in the idea or action you want them to follow.

Media Producers Just as our five senses are our guides in life, they can also be our enemies and traitors. Our sense of sight and the visual processing areas of the brain are compelling. We almost always dream visually, even if another sense is missing, and we usually picture someone we are remembering rather than associating some other sensory input with them. This makes imagery and visual manipulation an incredibly powerful technique of media mind control.

Traditionally, media production was in the hands of companies and institutions. These manipulative entities were able to pioneer the use of visual, subliminal mind control. Examples include split-second pictures of a product or person inserted into a seemingly innocent movie. Such splitsecond images, which the person perceives as nothing more than a flash of light, can take powerful control of a person's emotions. They have been used as recently as 21st-century Presidential elections.

Sound is another way in which a person is vulnerable to undetected mind control. Both experiments and personal experience will confirm this to you. Have you ever loved a song until it stuck in your head? How easy was it to get rid of? The sound had a powerful influence over you, even though you knew it was present. The power of audio manipulation is even greater when it is undetected. Experiments have shown that if restaurant customers are exposed to music from a particular region, they are more likely to order wine from that country. When questioned, they had no idea that something as simple as the sound had steered their decision.

Lovers People are always a product of the environment they are in. The way people are raised affects the way they act in later life. Someone raised by alcoholics has a greater chance of becoming alcoholics in adult life, or they may choose never to drink. People raised in a house where everything is prohibited may cut loose when they are finally on their own. People from different economic and religious backgrounds. People have different beliefs about what is right and wrong, what is acceptable and unacceptable. The problem comes when two people try to have a relationship, but neither wants to change their way of thinking. When that happens, there is no relationship. Just two people are living together under the same roof. People who create and keep good, mutually satisfactory relationships with others enjoy much more success than people who do not do this. The ability to grow and maintain honest relationships is easier for some people. Salespeople If a salesperson asks a regular customer to write a brief endorsement of the product they buy, they will hopefully say yes. If someone asks their significant other to take some of the business cards to pass out at work, they will hopefully say yes. If you write any blog and ask another blogger to provide a link to yours on their blog, they will hopefully say yes. When enough people say yes, the business or blog will begin to grow. With even more yesses, it will continue to grow and thrive. This is the very simple basis of marketing. Marketing is nothing more than using mind control to get other people to buy something or do something beneficial. And the techniques can easily be learned. Writers Think of writing a guest spot for someone else who has their blog. By sending in the entire manuscript first, there is a greater risk of rejection. Begin small. Send them a paragraph or two discussing them with the idea. Then outline the idea and send that in an email. Then write the complete draft you would like them to use and send it along. When asking a customer for a testimonial, start by asking for a few lines in an email. Then ask the customer to expand those few lines into a testimonial covering at least half a typed page. The customer will soon be ready for an hour-long webcast extolling the virtues of the product and your excellent customer service skills. Everything must have a deadline that exists. The critical word here is the word 'real.' Everyone has heard the salesperson who said to decide because the deal might not be available later or another customer was coming in, and they might get it. That is a total fabrication, and everyone knows it to be true. There are no impending other customers, and the deal is not going to disappear. There is no real sense of urgency involved. But everyone does it. There are too many situations where people are given a fake deadline by someone who thinks it will instill a great sense of urgency for completing the task. It is not only not useful but completely unneeded. It is a simple matter to create real urgency. Only leave free things available for a finite amount of time. When asking customers for testimonials, be sure to mention the last possible day for it to be received to be used.

Some people will be unable to assist but having people unable to participate is better than never beginning.

In Education By educating impressionable children, society essentially teaches them to become "ideal" members of the community. They are taught and trained in specific ways that fulfill the government and authorities' desires and don't even think twice about it. Advertising and Propaganda By putting advertising and propaganda everywhere, those in control can eliminate people's feelings of self-worth and encourage them to need what is being sold instead of just wanting it. This is essentially a subliminal strategy to make people feel poorly about themselves to purchase whatever is being advertised to increase their feelings of self-worth. Sports, Politics, Religion The idea of these strategies is to "divide and conquer." Ultimately, each one has people placed into various categories, where they feel very strongly. As a result, they don't support one another, but instead, they are against each other. This means that they are divided, and so the authority can conquer.

Chapter 21. The Process of Mind Control

A mind controller approaches the victim with the sole intent of cloning themselves, which is making the other person think like them. This is a complicated thing to do, so, to achieve it, one has to possess an inflated ego, lack doubts about themselves, and have a high sense of entitlement. All of us are susceptible to manipulation, and what matters is how much effect the mind control will have on us.

Psychologists studying mind control have found out that the entire process seems to adhere to a common structure. This conclusion was made after a study was conducted on multiple marketing and networking companies which used mind control to persuade clients to purchase their products. One of the outstanding similarities is that all new members joining the companies underwent a pre-planned training on how to recruit more people and convince potential customers to buy their products. The training sessions are meant to make the employees think like the company wants and use a form of mind twist to convince people.

Let us now look at the mind control process in detail.

Step 1 – Understanding the Target

Before anything else, the manipulator will seek to establish a bond or connection with their potential victim. Good intent, or friendship, will be the first step because it makes the victim lower all their social and psychological defenses. Once the controller gains the trust of the target, they now start reading them so as to devise the most effective method to invade them. The aim of the reading is to tell whether their victim is susceptible to their manipulation. Just like any project manager, they do not like wasting time on a subject they suspect might outsmart them and lead to failure.

There are multiple clues that are used to scan the victim. They include verbal style, body language, social status, gender, emotional stability, and so on. A person's traits can be used to decode the strength of their defenses. All this time, the manipulator will be asking themselves questions like, "Are you introvert or extrovert?" "Are you weakly?" "Are you emotional?" "Are you self-confident?" Humans give a lot of information about themselves when interacting with each other, and this is something that the controller knows all too well. From these signs, they can easily tell if the person is cooperating. They will look at body posture and immediately analyze the victim. Excess blinking might insinuate that a person is lying. Arms folded across the chest might show a lack of interest or insecurity. Taking large strides while walking might portray fear. As you can see, the body releases so much data at any given time that it is important to be aware of the signs that you are giving out.

When the attacker has collected enough data from the target, they now understand their interests, strengths, weaknesses, routines, and so on. Using this information, they can decide on an entry point which will allow for easy and accurate manipulation. They also decide whether the target is worth the effort. In the event that they see one as a favorable target, they move to the next step in the mind control processunfreezing solid beliefs and values.

Step 2- Unfreezing Solid Beliefs and Values

Each one of us has some beliefs and values engraved deep within. Most of them are the principles that were instilled in us since childhood, and others have been acquired from experiences are we grow older. We rarely let go of them but revise them as we proceed. Most of them are what make up our identities, so, we do not like them being interfered with. If at any point in time, these principles are threatened, contradicted, or questioned, our natural reaction is to defend them through all means possible. However, if a good-enough reason is given to us, so we voluntarily question them ourselves; we undergo a process known as "unfreezing." Tons of reasons can lead us to unfreeze: a breakup, the death of a loved one, religious interference, getting evicted from our houses, to mention but a few. These situations force us to start seeking answers to complex situations, and this goes as deep as questioning our sole beliefs and values. Take this, for example:

When I was a teenager, we had some family friends who were solid Christians. It so happened that my best friend, who was my exact age, came from this family. His name was Sam. Sam used to tell me about the Bible and its teachings, trying to convince me to accept salvation and live according to its teachings. I remember asking him why he was so insistent on this issue, and he would respond that with salvation, all problems were solvable, and that life was much easier and happier. Fast-forward about fifteen years, Sam's mother was diagnosed with breast cancer. They tried all forms of treatment available at the time, but cancer would grow back. One day, while talking to him about the issue, he looked at me with a pale face and said, "I think what they say about Christianity is not real!" Unsure about what he had just said, I asked him why he thought so. His response was that they had met tens of spiritual leaders for prayers, but his mother's cancer was only getting worse. What's worse; she would not live for more than a year.

Sad as Sam's story is, it makes us realize that some situations in life might force us to question the strong principles that we grow up with. In this case, my best friend had come to doubt the very same religion that he once felt had automatic solutions to all of life's problems. In the very same manner, a manipulator will dig deep in their victim's life to understand their vulnerabilities and exploit them fully. These people will say anything they think their targets would love to hear. Once the victim swallows the manipulator's comfort, there is a shift in power dynamics, and the target is now ready for the manipulation.

Step 3 – Reprogramming the Mind

The mind control process seeks to separate the target from their initial beliefs and begin reprogramming their mind. The reprogramming is meant to install the manipulator's beliefs and values into the victim's mind. Apart from distancing the initial principles, the controller also tries their best to make them look wrong or bad, or the cause of past mishaps in the victim's life. If the victim absorbs this reprogramming, their defense is literally lowered to zero, and they now become a robot that is ready to accept any operating system that is offered.

During the reprogramming phase, the attacker will try to ensure the victim has minimal contact with the outside world. They make everyone else to appear insignificant to the victim because this raises their opportunity to deposit their malicious principles into them. This behavior is common in cults, which are mostly crafted to sway their followers from mainstream human life. Some cults go as far as controlling the food intake of their followers as a way of weakening them. The psychology behind this idea is that a weak person will always turn to the person they feel has the power to protect them or alleviate their suffering. The same happens in relationships, where one partner plays the controlling role, and the victimized one has no choice but to adhere to the other. You might wonder why some people put up with violent partners, but so far, from reading this guidebook, you must already understand that the problem is deeper than it appears. If you control a person's mind, you can control their lives. Once the victim has been re-programmed, the manipulator moves into the final phase of the mind control process known as "freezing."

Step 4 – Freezing the New Beliefs and Values

Do you remember the "unfreezing" process we discoursed earlier? So, once the victim has been fed with contrasting principles by the offender, the offender applies tactics aimed at cementing the new beliefs into their brains. This is what psychologists call "freezing." The freezing bit is necessary because the controller is aware of the person's new beliefs that might clash with their initial ones. As such, they need to force the victim to choose their malicious principles over their old ones. To do this, they might apply any of the following methods.

One of the methods is using the reward/punishment approach. When the victim acts according to the manipulator's demands, they are rewarded. Hopefully, you see the similarity between the freezing process and dog training. The dog is given treats when it follows the trainer's instructions. The trainer aims at solidifying the new skill in the dog by rewarding it. In the future, if the dog is instructed to do the same thing, it will not hesitate since it has been made to think that obeying the command is good and attracts a reward. The same applies to mind control; when the victim obeys, they are made to feel that what they did was right and deserves a reward.

Punishments are the second most-applied approach in the freezing process. If the victim deviates from the controller's commands, they are punished. If we go back to the scenario of a cult, they usually have defined punishments for violations of terms. During the Holocaust, for instance, any Germans who failed to hail Hitler were punished through imprisonment or death. In the same way, any German who was suspected of protecting the Jews was shot. Hitler understood that by punishing anyone who went against his rules, he would force every German to help him attain his objective of ethnic cleansing. The psychological trick used in these situations is that the victim is made to see punishment as justice being served for breaking the rules.

The final method used by mind controllers to solidify their manipulation is to transform their victims into their agents. Better put, once the controller feels that the victim's pseudo personality has materialized, they use them to distribute their worldviews. At the beginning of this guidebook, we said that the agenda of the mind controller is to create a replica of themselves in the other person. Therefore, once the controlling process is complete, the victim starts living like the attacker without realizing it. Depending on the nature of the manipulation, the victim might also be used to recruit more victims into the oppressor's way of thinking and living This is especially true in the context of marketing and networking, which we shall discuss under the topic of deception. From this explanation, we can readily tell why a wife is likely to be violent towards the kids if the husband is violent. The kids are also likely to be violent towards each other or their friends. Clearly, the process of mind

control is slow, but once it solidifies, it can result in devastating
effects.

Chapter 22.Brainwashing

Brainwashing as a manipulation technique is far more powerful than both mind control and hypnosis, but it also requires far more training and expertise to be used most efficiently. While many of the concepts used in hypnosis and mind control overlap with brainwashing, there are also new techniques made available to you when you learn about brainwashing. Like hypnosis, brainwashing is a popular topic and plot device in many books, movies, and other media. Of course, as being the most powerful technique, brainwashing is also more high-profile than hypnosis and mind control. It has been used extensively in certain largescale scenarios, including by certain governments, cults, corporations, etc. While brainwashing has been known throughout history by many different names, including thought reform, thought control, coercive persuasion, and re-education for the sake of simplicity, this will only refer to it as brainwashing.

By learning more about what brainwashing is and how it works, you will not only have gained a valuable technique for manipulating other people, but you will also be able to more easily recognize when you are being brainwashed by another person or by an organization.

The History of Brainwashing One of the most well-known portrayals of brainwashing on a massive scale in fiction is found in the book 1984, which was written by George Orwell in 1949. In the book, a massive government entity maintains complete control over its citizens by creating propaganda, using surveillance to spy on people, rationing food, and even training people to use a different language.

There is no magical technology that allows the government to control its citizens' thoughts and actions directly. Still, through the laws it creates and how it enforces those laws, it can make its citizens think and act in only the ways that it wants them to.

Even though 1984 is a work of fiction, governments like the one described in the book have certainly existed in real life and continue to do so today. Of course, brainwashing has been used by other organizations than governments in its history, and different groups have used brainwashing successfully in different ways to further their goals.

While certain forms of brainwashing techniques have been in use for thousands of years, the public did not become aware of brainwashing on a large scale until the 1940s and the 1950s.

At that time, brainwashing was a major part of society in China under Mao Zedong, the Chairman of the Communist Party of China and China's leader overall. The term "brainwashing" comes from the Chinese phrase xi[nǎo, which translates to "wash brain" in English. Americans were not made aware of brainwashing as a phenomenon until after the Korean War had begun. During the war, American soldiers were captured as prisoners of war (POWs), and during their time spent in Chinese prison facilities, they were brainwashed by the Chinese government. The POWs that had been brainwashed were more likely to give over classified information to the Chinese and give false confessions, more willing to do what their captors wanted them to, and even defended the Chinese government's actions.

The United Nations commander at the time stated that "too familiar are the mind-annihilating methods of these Communists in forcing whatever words they want...The men themselves are not to be liable and they have my deepest compassion for having been used in this awful way." In other words, the Chinese were extremely skilled at brainwashing their victims, who would feel the effects of being brainwashed for years after it had been done to them. After American POWs were found to have been brainwashed, the United States Central Intelligence Agency (CIA) ran a series of experiments over twenty years that tested mind control and brainwashing capabilities, the most famous of these experiments being called Project MKUltra. To testing general brainwashing techniques, the CIA also experimented with drugs as a tool for manipulation and attempted to create a so-called truth serum that would be used for interrogation purposes.

From there, brainwashing took hold in the public's minds and began to play a large part in popular culture. Large audiences received stories involving brainwashing, and movies such as The Fear makers, Toward the Unknown, The Bamboo Prison, The Rack, and The Manchurian Candidate were all inspired in some part by the experience of American POWs during the war or brainwashing in general. Starting in the late 1960s and extending through the mid-1970s, brainwashing as a concept was so deeply rooted in the public consciousness that it even seeped into the criminal justice system. Perhaps the most famous example is Patty Hearst, an heiress who was kidnapped and brainwashed by a terrorist group known as the Symbionese Liberation Army (SLA). She later joined the group as a member and was arrested during an attempted bank robbery.

Her trial was the first widely publicized instance of using brainwashing as a legal defense in court. While she was ultimately found guilty, the defense caused a renewal of interest and concern over brainwashing.

Since the 1960s, brainwashing has also been widely used in recruiting members to cults. The most well-known instance of brainwashing being used in cults is probably that of the Manson Family, founded in 1967 by Charles Manson. Manson was an extremely skilled manipulator, and successfully recruited nearly

100 people, mostly women, into his cult following. He had such a strong influence over them that he was able to convince them to commit several different crimes, from assault and robbery to mass murder. Nearly all cults use some form of brainwashing to influence potential recruits and convince them to join, from the most infamous to cults you have never heard of before. Some cults, such as Heaven's Gate and The People's Temple, used brainwashing to such a powerful effect that their followers were convinced to commit suicide.

Cults are especially important to study brainwashing because they demonstrate how far the power of brainwashing techniques can take people and are a good indicator of when things have gone too far. Suppose you are thinking of using brainwashing or any other manipulation on a person to make them inflict harm on themselves or anyone else. In that case, you should refrain from doing so and seek professional help for yourself.

But why is the history of brainwashing so important to learn about? After all, you are not a government entity such as the Communist Party of China, and you are hopefully not planning on dabbling in becoming a cult leader of any kind. Of course, there are valuable lessons to be learned from the history of brainwashing that you can apply to how you approach and implement brainwashing techniques in your own life. First of all, having a great understanding of brainwashing history should mean that you also have a good understanding of just how powerful brainwashing can be, even on the most unwilling targets. If American soldiers can be brainwashed into defending their captors, the country's enemies that they vowed to serve, then imagine what brainwashing can do for you if used correctly. Secondly, brainwashing history teaches the important lesson that anybody and everybody are susceptible to brainwashing techniques unlike mind control and hypnosis. If you focus on honing your talents and become a skilled enough manipulator, you can brainwash not just one person, but multiple people at a time into doing whatever it is that you want for them to do. The most talented manipulators can exert their influence over hundreds of people all at once, and every single one of their targets will be as thoroughly taught as the last one. This leads me into the final reason why the history of brainwashing is important to have at least some knowledge of because brainwashing is such a powerful and effective tool that can be used on so many people, it can be easy to take brainwashing too far, and force your targets into criminal or even life-threatening situations. By studying brainwashing history, you will know how horrible the effects of brainwashing can be for the target, the manipulator, and for anybody else who gets caught in between.

While brainwashing as a tactic is not in and of itself harmful, when used with reckless abandon, things can quickly spiral out of control. As the manipulator, it is your responsibility to know when to stop before something terrible has occurred. Above all else, brainwashing history demonstrates the need to be safe, sensible, and responsible when using brainwashing techniques, as the consequences can be dire if brainwashing is used irresponsibly.

Chapter 23. 10 Steps of Brainwashing

Brainwashing phrases are mostly separate and can be generally divided into three levels. The first stage involves all the methods the abuser takes to tear down their prey; the second phase requires convincing the prey that there is a possibility of redemption; and lastly, the 3rd stage is where the target redeems itself and embraces his new self.

First Stage: Breaking the Target

Step 1: Identity Assaulting

To break down a predator's target, they may be the first target that makes the victim what they are: their ego or identity. Each human being has in his mind an idea of himself which is what they claim to be. This is the way they define themselves. Multiple identities are possible. You could be a mother and a career woman. You may be a smart businessman and an uncle. You may be a hard-fought student at the class. You just might be a Christian. You can choose between endless identities. That identity is your solution to the declaration tell me about yourself a little bit. Suppose one day you wake up and someone advised you that you're not really what you believe you are. How do you manage to hear that? If this was deliberated in passing, you should possibly shrug it off and go on with your career. Or maybe you'd worry about it for a few hours or minutes, and maybe get frustrated for a bit, then push on. Now imagine someone comes to your home every minute of the day to remind you that you're not the guy you believe you are. How'd that help you feel? If it lasted through months or even weeks, then you will be out of your head by the end of it. You will be startled and left to question where to distinguish between fiction and fact.

If you'd thought about yourself as a great writer before, you'd start to doubt it. If you thought you were your children's biological father, you may start questioning him. If you've grown up thinking you're a real catholic, hearing daily contradictory reports would make you start thinking you might not be.

The first phase in the brainwashing cycle is when the entire dirty work starts taking hold. An individual who has planted the ugly seed of doubt in them is endangered to manipulation. We want to think the best of ourselves, as human beings. Also, we like having other people believe in us the best. Yes, some individuals may not care about someone else's validation and approval. That's admirable and we should all be working towards that. But at the last of the day, the guy who goes to bed thinking he is the worst of the bad periods of sleep more restlessly. Having high self-esteem and a strong sense of self, of course, saves you from the predators willing to attack you.

The result of the first phase of brainwashing is a completelyblown identity issue which the predator could prey on for the second step's purposes.

Step 2: Guilt Manipulation

Guilt, as it's been called, maybe a negative emotion, it is also a quite strong feeling. Guilt can start making you, as a person, promise things outside of your scope. Guilt will make you sit awake for hours wondering if you're such a bad human being because you're not. The human creatures around us are continually harnessing the strength of liability.

This is how the second phase of brainwashing tends to work: a brainwasher has indeed convinced its victim that they're not really what they've always assumed to be. Hence, the survivor is in a state of uncertainty because they try to address the issue of identification. Such that, if they aren't a decent guy, why are they then? The predator glides in at this point and begins to take them for their lives' entire sorrow trip. When you're uncertain who you are, it can be tempting to accept every falsehood you're getting fed up with about you. A brainwasher would also make a statement convincing their perpetrator that they are a nasty friend, irrespective of how this adverb is being used.

Steps 3 and 4: Personality-betrayal and breaking point

Even citizens themselves are intensely loyal. They're going to protect themselves and their behavior, and struggle to hear their words. Particularly the individuals who are afraid of speaking up for anyone also will speak up for themselves. A person having been brainwashed is the total opposite. Brainwashed people have no trouble rejecting themselves and anything else connected to them despite being continuously bombarded by signals about being the reverse about what they once considered themselves to be. This involves their family, associates, value framework, and all other relationships they might have that link them to the old identification that has been 'evaluated' by the brainwasher and found 'seriously missing.'

There are several reasons why a person who has been brainwashed can easily find himself in this step and cannot fight back. For beginners, they've already moved through the first 2 phases and come out in doubt and guilt, feeling drowning and disoriented. But frequently they don't have the strength to strike off. Remember that there is sometimes a risk of serious harm if conformance is not accomplished, so the goal may be too scared to contradict all the predator's replies.

Second Stage: Dangling a Salvation Carrot

Step 5: The Olive Branch After

the first 3 stages of brainwashing, a survivor of brainwashing sometimes feels so bad about themselves because they try to save themselves at whatever expense. The survivor is also in bad emotional health and has a weak selfimage. Those who have forgotten their longtime sense of belonging and will clutch up on any straws offered to feel

something again. At this stage, a victim becomes expected to experience a nervous collapse, and that is the signal for the attacker to leap in and deliver redemption.

The manipulator would also offer an olive branch after tearing down their objective for a long period so that the goal will slip into the pit of thinking there is hope at the last of a tunnel. An olive branch at this point could be something from a sweet word to a gift, or perhaps even some type of personal affection. This olive branch helps to demonstrate the goal that there is certain leniency to gain when they're on the right side of the manipulator. A manipulator is above all a 'normal guy' who wishes them the best. That is at least what they have learned since the start of brainwashing.

Step 6: Being Forced to Confess Take into account:

You have been confined for an amount of time to intense mental abuse by an individual. You have wasted your sense of belonging and feel confused and angry. You 're facing a psychotic collapse or already experienced one and can't make every part of your life head or tails. Since leaving the social network you have existed in solitary isolation and can't think of the last moment you had such a decent meal. Then, one day, this individual comes up at your door carrying a steaming coffee pot and freshly prepared muffins. They just say they want to chat. You are inviting them to your building. You just can't believe it. It's the only love you've been receiving in the longest period. What do you believe your former abuser will be reacting to this unusual kindness?

You'll experience a sense of sovereign debt more often than not. Human beings enjoy being kind enough to reciprocate that compassion. Whenever somebody does something good for you, then in exchange, it is natural and wants to do anything better. For a brainwashed human, the desire to pay back is much greater as they believe they still have to compensate for anything they are incorrect about. The brainwashed side, therefore, will be more than willing to offer away some type of kindness. This goodness would always come in the shape of a lie, in their troubled minds. The perpetrator would usually give the alternative of an apology as a means to get paid back.

Step 7: Guilt Channeling

A brainwashed survivor is frequently filled by so much crushing remorse that they still have no scope for any other feeling after weeks or months of becoming told they 're mistaken on anything. The goal has been swamped by so much abuser psychological torment they don't realize what we feel most bad for. The victim simply knows he's guilty of anything. In this misunderstanding, the manipulator glides in and persuades them that guilt is due to all the bad people they've believed in before. The predator, in other words, streams the guilt into the system of belief. The victim now begins to associate their beliefs with the guilt and the responsibility of dealing with the guilt. By fact, the abuser wants to help their prey continue to equate all the negative emotions of their history and let them think that if they select different values, there is a possibility to be rescued and feel stronger.

Step 8: Guilt Relief

The victim is beginning to feel a little relieved to recognize that he's just not deeply bad; perhaps, it is his perceptions that are wrong. He can be correct again, by detaching himself from his beliefs. He sheds his remorse by relinquishing anything related to his prejudices, even those nearest to him. He admits the mistakes of his previous ways and can embark on the current set of values that the brainwasher provides.

Third Stage: Reconstruction of a Brainwashed Self

Step 9: Harmony and Progress

At this stage in brainwashing, the target is keen to redeem itself and look very good in the brainwasher's eyes. Even so, they will start rebuilding a new identity based on the manipulator's offered belief system. After passing through the torture and suffering of the early phases of brainwashing, an offender is assured that only pain and guilt will come from their old belief system. They are glad to be rid of the former life and replaced with a new self that is their safe place from all their suffering.

Step 10: Rebirth and Final Confession

The survivor also experiences a sense of satisfaction upon embracing the current moral structure to be finished for their history and all of the resulting pain. Like the stereotypical last rope on a sinking ship, they must stick to their new identities as this is the only happiness they have experienced in a long period. At this stage, the brainwasher succeeded in obtaining a conversion, and might even be conducting a ritual to invite the latest conversion into the holy inner circle. It is typical for the majority of offenders to be separated from their families. They're going to get it in their heads that they're better individuals today and don't have to deal with their previous negative stuff.

Chapter 24.How to Protect Yourself from Becoming A Victim of Dark Psychology Manipulation

Protection is always better than cure. There is some depth of Dark psychology that you cannot afford to disentangle yourself from without external help. This external help is not always guaranteed. Thus, the best way is to guard yourself.

The following are the main steps to protect yourself from becoming a victim of Dark psychology:

⏹ Use White psychology tools to your advantage

⏹ Learn to detect Dark psychology predators

⏹ Avoid becoming a Dark psychology prey

⏹ Form an army of defense against Dark psychology predators

Use the White Psychology Tools to Your Advantage

The following are very important White psychology tools that you can use to protect yourself from becoming a victim of Dark Psychology:

⏹ Mindfulness meditation

⏹ Neuro-Linguistic Programming (NLP)

⏹ Neuroplasticity

⏹ Power Posing

▢ Positive Thinking and Positive Affirmation

▢ Creative Visualization

How to use mindfulness meditation to protect yourself from Dark psychology predators

Mindfulness is about becoming self-aware. Those who are not self-aware become easy prey to be devoured by the Dark psychology predators. Like all predators, there is a predator that can eat every other kind of meat. Thus, predators select their prey depending on certain traits. These are the traits you have to avoid. Lack of self-awareness is the great trait of a Dark psychology prey.

We know that Dark psychology predators create psychological traps within your mind. Being self-aware enables you to see these traps... be they in terms of thoughts, ideas, etc. Being able to detect these traps means that you cannot be ensnared.

Meditation is a powerful tool that blends so well with mindfulness. Meditation is about focusing and concentration.

More often than not, Dark psychology preys are never focused. Their mind wanders from one thought proposal to another and seeks to cling on every other attractive thought. In essence, their minds are promiscuous and lack fidelity to held thoughts.

It is this mind-wandering that becomes susceptible to traps of alien thoughts that are manipulative.

By pushing you to concentrate and focus on what matters, you are able to avoid veering off from your core mindset into the traps of the mindset of the Dark psychology preys.

How to Use NLP To Protect Yourself from Dark Psychology Predators NLP is inevitably a powerful tool.

If there is a tool that can be used by Dark psychology predators to be devastating effect, then it is NLP. Yet, the same tool can be used to fend off these preys by those who know how to use them. NLP is both an arming and disarming tool.

NLP is more important in overcoming negative self-image which leads to low self-esteem.

Low self-esteem is a very powerful magnetic attraction to Dark psychology predators. It is like a powerful scent of meat to them. It raises their raw appetite to extreme levels of greed. It scintillates their gnashing jaws. Like crocodiles, they will come crashing at their prey like no mercy exists on this earth.

You can use NLP to remap your mind such that that the mental maps no longer point to the negative images. Instead, replacing the meaning of meta tags from negative to positive can trigger a counter-negative effect.

How to use neuroplasticity to protect yourself from Dark psychology predators

You can take advantage of how the brain works so as to effectively utilize resources in order to rewire it away from those things that no longer serve your best interest.

For example, seduction is the most potent weapon for emotional manipulation. More often than not, Dark psychology predators use sexual or sensual seduction to trap their preys. Through neuroplasticity, you can rewire your mind such that it adapts learned non-use of certain sensual cues that are commonly susceptible to Dark seductive predators.

How to use power posing to protect yourself from Dark psychology predators

One important trait of a Dark psychology prey is lack of selfconfidence. Lack of self-confidence emanates from low selfesteem triggered by having a negative self-image. We've seen how NLP can be used to rewire your mind's meta tags away from a negative self-image. However, NLP, on its own may not bring out that external aspect that scares away predators.

Like in the wild, we understand how a self-confident dominant posture can help one scare away potential predators.

A predator is very calculative. A predator calculates the risks versus rewards of pouncing on potential prey. Instinctively, if the risks are such high such that the predator more likely to be crushed rather than have a meal, then, the predator will not dare such a potentially fatal adventure.

Thus, having a self-confident dominant posture helps to ward off potential Dark psychology predators.

Power posing is about using your body posture to bring out this self-confident dominant posture.

Some of the most potent Power posing postures include:

• Looking at the potential Predator straight and sharply in the eyes. This will weaken and keep off deceptive characters

• Looking bold and emotionless – this will weaken and keep off seductive characters

• Portraying a straight, upright, and bold posture – this will keep off narcissistic psychopaths who are most adept at employing bullying tactics to push their victims into submission and perpetual surrender

How to use Positive thinking and Positive affirmations to protect yourself from Dark psychology predators

Like mindfulness and meditation, positive thinking and positive affirmation are two different tools. However, they are more potent when they are combined together.

Positive thinking and positive affirmation reinforce each other in a cyclical way such as to have greater force and amplitude.

Yet, mindfulness meditation, NLP, and neuroplasticity are very important sharpening tools for both positive thinking and positive affirmation. They make positive thinking and positive affirmations to become real rather than the vacuous mind posturing.

The following are some of the ways you can employ a combination of positive thinking and positive affirmation to conquer Dark psychology predators:

When a dark predator casts you in a negative light — the aim is to push you into self-doubt. Your response could be:

Positive thinking: I know what this man wants. I am not what he says I am.

Positive affirmation: I am complete and wonderfully made

How to use Creative visualization to protect yourself from Dark psychology predators

We've also seen how Dark Psychology manipulators plant negative self-image in their victims so as to drive them into a state of low self-esteem – a state which is definitely their home ground.

Creative visualization, like NLP, can enable you to focus on the right self-image and thus avoid the negative self-image that does not fit into your reality.

You can use Creative visualization to create a self-image of what you would like to be in the future. For example:

• A successful career wife or husband

• A successful free-willed entrepreneur

• An independent-minded tough optimist

Once you have created this image, you live it as if you are already in it. It is like creating a blueprint of your desired house, and then feel yourself living in it. In your mind, you are actually living in it... right now! You are not projecting to live in it in the future once you have physically built it. No! You remove that disconnect that is so-called "future" from that image. You can use NLP's dissociative tool, to get rid of that "future" disconnect.

This way, there is no possibility that a narcissistic psychopath or sadist can come and tell you "Your homeless creature, you are worth nothing. Take what I am offering you (as my sex object in my house) as something better than your nothingness".

Yes, without that mental image you've created of a decent respectful home for your being, you are more likely to descend into low self-esteem at the crushing boots of a narcissistic psychopath.

Creative visualization helps you avoid becoming a victim of Dark psychology preys.

Through creative visualization, you are able to create an alternative reality. Not a fake one, but a real one because you are able to focus your attention and energy towards its gradual realization.

Creative visualization is not about fantasies. It is about "still arriving". You are living in the image you have created and working to actualize it each and every moment of that livelihood. It is like playing a video. You cannot see every scene at once. Step by step, a frame comes and you are able to see it. The frames flow in a seamless continuous pattern such that you forget that actually there are hundreds and even thousands of images flowing to create this movie. Isn't it possible that you can continually create more frames as you are watching the current ones unveil? Yes, that's what episodes are all about.

Creative visualization is about creating episodes of your movie of life. You live it as it unveils. You live it as you create more scenes and pack them into frames. There is no waiting. You are not trapped in that waiting called "future". You are living in the current episode and still arriving in the next episode. There is no disconnect in your movie of life. Why would you afford to be distracted? Don't!

Be able to detect dark predators The survival of every other prey depends on how it is able to detect its predators. This is the first and most paramount step of survival for the fittest.

Obviously, every day a predator survives is a testimony that a prey lost its survival. If you are alive, then, it simply means you have survived long enough to witness the predator alive. To continue being alive, you have to continue being alert.

To be able to detect a predator, you must have: • A clear image of the nature of your predator

• Clear attributes that help you detect this image

• Properly profile your predator

• Avoid becoming a dark prey

It is natural that there will exist preys and predators. But it is also natural that some potential preys can avoid becoming victims of predators and thus live a full life.

Regardless of the sheer number of Dark psychology predators, a lot of them disguised, you can avoid becoming their prey.

The following are things you must do to avoid becoming the next prey:

• Be ever consciously alert and vigilant — you can only detect predators by being consciously alert. We've seen how mindfulness meditation can help in this regard.

• Sharpening your self-defense mechanism — even with optimal alertness, it is natural that there are moments you go to sleep... for your brain to relax and your mind to replenish. It is at such moments that you become susceptible. Like the powerful gores of a buffalo or the fatal kicks of a giraffe, you can give a predator a testimony that it will never forget... that is, if it happens to survive. This means that you must equip yourself with powerful defensive tools just in case you are inadvertently caught.

• Be quick to act fast and swift — What saves an antelope from becoming a leopard's next meal is its ability to be quick, fast and swift in its response. Similarly, your flight mechanism should be optimal.

Chapter 25.Mind Games

Mind games may be something that you think you understand and can recognize in your daily life. And it is probably true that someone has tried to play these games on you, and you were able to catch on to them. However, a real manipulator can use these mind games in a way that can build up sympathy for themselves, without the victim ever realizing what is going on.

It is common to attribute a lot of normal behaviors to mind games. The intentions of the person who uses genuinely dark mind games are never friendly, positive, or good. Therefore, these innocent games, like surprises and teasing, will not fit this category right from the beginning.

Mind games are going to be any psychological scheme on behalf of a manipulator towards their victim.

A dark mind game is often one that the manipulator is just going to play for their delight or their amusement. The

manipulator isn't going to have any regard for the wellbeing of the victim.

What is the motivation behind these dark mind games?

The motivation behind the mind game can make the difference in whether it is seen as something positive or dark psychology. The range of motivations that come with these manipulative mind games will be determined based on what the manipulator wants to do and who their victim is at the time.

The manipulator may feel that the other forms of manipulation are not all that effective, and they may try to use something less obvious to their target, such as a mind game. It also can influence the victim in this way just because it amuses them and not because they are trying to gain something out of the manipulation.

The specific types of influences that can be gained from playing these types of mind games will be explored here in a bit. But basically, these mind games are useful to a manipulator because they will reduce the amount of certainty that the victim has, and the psychological strength that the manipulator gains are very subtle and hard to see.

Many times, these mind games will be used to achieve influence while maintaining the illusion of autonomy with that victim.

Influencing a victim is not the only motivation behind someone using mind games. Many manipulators will choose to play these mind games to entertain themselves. They like and get pleasure from plotting out ways to impact the victim's psychology, and they enjoy watching the victim succumb to their intentions. This is similar to what a sociopath may do. The manipulator will not see the other person, their victim, as someone who has feelings and thoughts.

Sometimes, the dark mind games are played because they are learned behavior rather than as a manipulator's conscious intent. This is when the manipulative individual has been exposed to these mind games throughout their life, and they don't know how to act in any other way. This may seem innocent, but it can be just as dangerous because they learned how to act this way and have developed even more methods to trick their victims into behaving a certain way.

Some Methods Used in Mind Games Now that you know a bit more about the differences between regular mind games and dark mind games, it is time to explore the different types of mind games that a manipulator can use. The specific games can sometimes have innocent variants in them, but sometimes these variants are dark. Let's take a look at the different types of mind games that a manipulator may try to employ to get what they want from their victim.

Ultimatums An ultimatum is when one person can present the other with a severe choice. It will often take the form of demand, such as "Do this... or this will happen." Some examples of how this may play out include:

"Lose weight...or I will see other people." ▨

"Quit smoking...or I will leave you." 🄯

Ultimatums are like a request, but it has turned itself more into demand. They pretty much leave the victim without any choice in the manner. With the example above, the other person will have to lose weight or be with the person they

love any longer. They either need to quit smoking, or the other person is going to leave them. If the victim states that these ultimatums leave them with no choices, the manipulator can always come back and state that the victim had a choice, even though the manipulator knows this isn't true.

Three factors are going to determine if the ultimatum is considered dark psychology. First is the type of person who gives the ultimatum, the other person's intention when giving the ultimatum, and the nature of the request or the ultimatum itself.

First, let's look at the person who is giving the ultimatum. If the ultimatum is legitimate, then the person who gives it may have a valid and genuine care about the person they want to help. They may say something like, "Lose weight...or you are going to end up with a lot of health problems in the future." There is still an ultimatum because something will happen to the victim, but they aren't saying it to mean or take away love and care for the other person.

The motivation that comes with that ultimatum will be another important element of how you can understand it.

Those who issue ultimatums with some good intentions will do it because they want to help make something better in the other person's life. These ultimatums will be issues with the intention and the purpose of helping the other person make a good choice and make positive life changes.

Judging these ultimatums' intentions can be difficult, which is sometimes why it is so hard to figure out if the ultimatum is dark or not. But with dark ultimatums, the request is often going to go against what is in the victim's best self-interest.

The Eternal Breakup One of the fundamental requirements for a good romantic relationship is that both parties need to feel contentment and security. People in happy romances or happy marriages will feel at ease and will not deal with a constant threat that the relationship will end at any time. Masters of manipulation understand these principles and will do everything in their power to invert them. By cultivating a sense of negativity, chaos, and instability in the relationship, the manipulator can keep their victim powerless for a long time.

The eternal breakup is the prolonged and persistent use of threatening to leave someone. This could be a promise, an implied, or an actual breakup that is never followed.

With an implied breakup, they will not involve the overt mention of the breaking up. The manipulator will hint at the breakup to put some doubt in their victim's mind. The manipulator may casually mention plans, ones that don't involve the victim at all. They may even decide to hint at an active breakup by saying something like, "Well, I won't put up with that for long" or another veiled hint. Any sentence or action that could make the victim doubt if the relationship will last can be counted as an implied breakup.

There is also a promised breakup. This is a step between the two types of breakups. This will happen when the manipulator issues a threat to their victim and then overtly states that they intend to break up with their victim in the future. The manipulator may resort to saying something like, "I am going to leave you soon, and then I won't have to deal with this anymore." Any Instance where the manipulator brings up the idea of a divorce, separation, or breakup, but they don't carry out this step will be a good example of the promised breakup.

Then there is the actual breakup that never occurs. This is the most severe option with the eternal breakup mind game. This is where the manipulator is going to break up with their victim without following through with it. They may decide to pack their bags and leave, recognize that the victim is sad or uncomfortable, and then not follow through with it. They may even break up with the victim, without any intention of following through. They will then "accept" the victim back after the victim shows enough sadness or beginning.

This tactic works because the victim has often been used and manipulated by the other partner for some time. They are often vulnerable and susceptible to the influence and the power of the manipulator. This makes them more eager to preserve the relationship, even though it has only a dark psychological playground that is fun for the manipulator but hard on the victim each day. If this type of mind game goes on for a long time, it can result in the victim developing trust issues and other options that are not so good for the victim's health.

Hard to Get This is another one that can be part of normal and healthy behavior, but then it can also be a part of dark psychology. An example of a hard to get mind game would be the following: a person wants to seem like they are a bit of a challenge to someone they are interested in. They will decide not to be available all the time. This may involve them not accepting every suggested date, taking their time to reply to calls and messages, and other behaviors. The intention here is to make sure that the other person stays interested, and it can help give them a happy and healthy relationship together.

But the dark psychological use of hard to get can be a lot more dangerous. Those who use this as a form of manipulation will play hard to get games at times other than at the beginning of the relationship. Their intention is not going to lead to a positive situation, and they don't care about the wellbeing of the other person. When this continues onto the later parts of the relationship, it can result in a manipulator in the unreliable and very evasive relationship.

This does not happen when a dark manipulator uses the hard to get mind games against one of their victims in a relationship.

When a person decides to play the hard to get mind game later on in the relationship, it will put the victim on the defensive, and they will need to put in some extra work. The victim will work hard to reconnect with the manipulator, who seems to be pulling away from them.

The point of this is that all this work on the part of the victim will gratify the manipulator's ego and can place the power back in their hands. The professional manipulators can balance out the actions that make them hard to get with those that convey some reliability and closeness. And when they do this successfully, it will lead to a lot of deep psychological confusion and even some instability in the mind of the victim. This allows the manipulator to get in there and exploit the situation in any manner they would like, without the victim realizing.

There are many different mind games that a manipulator can play against their victim.

Chapter 26. Tips to read and analyze people

Take a moment to imagine a time when the sight of someone sent a chill down your spine. You may not have known why, but you were simply uncomfortable around the person that you were facing. Despite your best attempts to identify the reasoning behind your problem, you found that there was no particular reason that you could discern. The only thing you knew was that you were the only thing afraid of the person in front of you and had no idea how to overcome them.

There was a very good reason for this guttural reaction—your instincts were telling you that something about the other person was not right. You didn't need to know specifics, and all that mattered to you was that your reactions were accurate. This is because all these guttural reactions must do keep you alive. So long as that is managed, your instincts did their job.

There are limitless reasons that being able to rationally understand what is going on in someone else's mind is critical, even if you already have a decent gut reaction. Ultimately, when you can analyze someone calmly and consciously be aware of why you are uncomfortable or what is putting you on-edge, you are better prepared to cope with the problem at hand. This is because you can act rationally. You can strategize on how to better react in the most conducive manner that will allow you to succeed in the situation.

This means that in the modern world, when things are very rarely life or death situations, making an effort to switch to responding rationally and consciously is almost always the best bet. You will be able to tell when someone is setting off your alarm bells because they seem threatening, or because they seem deceptive. You will be able to find out what the problem is to respond appropriately.

Why Analyze People Analyzing people is something that is utilized by several people in different capacities. The most basic reason you may decide that you wish to analyze someone is to understand them. When you have an in-built technique of understanding others, you will discover that having a cognitive instead of an emotional connection is critical to establishing a true connection with someone else's mind.

Consider for a moment that you are trying to land a deal with a very important client. You know that the deal is critical if you hope to keep your job and possibly even get a promotion, but you also know that it is going to be a difficult task to manage. If you can read someone else, you can effectively allow yourself the ability to know what is going on in their mind truly.

Think about it—you will be able to tell if the client is uncomfortable and respond accordingly. You will be able to tell if the client is being deceptive or withholding something —and respond accordingly. You can tell if the client is uninterested, feeling threatened, or even just annoyed with your attempts to sway him or her, and you can then find out how to reply.

When you can understand the mindset of someone else, you can self-regulate. You can fine-tune your behaviors to guarantee that you will be persuasive. You can make sure that your client feels comfortable by being able to adjust your behavior to find out what was causing the discomfort in the first place.

Beyond just being able to self-regulate, being able to read other people is critical in several other situations as well. If you can read someone else, you can protect yourself from any threats that may arise. If you can read someone else, you can simply understand their position better. You can find out how to persuade or manipulate the other person. You can get people to do things that they would otherwise avoid.

Ultimately, being able to analyze other people has so many critical benefits that it is worthwhile to be able to do so. Developing this skill set means that you will be more in touch with the feelings of those around you, allowing you to assert that you have a higher emotional intelligence simply because you come to understand what emotions look like. You will be able to identify your own emotions through self-reflection and to learn to pay attention to your body movements. The ability to analyze people can be invaluable in almost any setting.

How to Analyze People   Though it may sound intimidating, learning to analyze other people is not nearly as difficult as it may initially seem. There are no complicated rules that you need to memorize or any skills that you need to learn—all you have to do is learn the pattern of behaviors and what they mean. This is because once you know the behaviors; you can usually start to piece together the intent behind the behaviors.

You can begin to find out exactly what it is that someone's eyes narrowing means and then begin to identify it with the context of several other actions or behaviors as well. You can find out what is intended when someone's speech and their body language do not match up. Body language rarely lies when people are unaware of how it works, so you can often turn to it for crucial information if you are interacting with other people.

The reason this works to understand people is because it is commonly accepted that there is a cycle between thoughts, feelings, and behaviors. Your thoughts create feelings, and the feelings you have automatically influence your behaviors, as you can see through body language.

Effectively, you will be looking at behaviors that people display and then tracing them back to the feelings behind them. This is why body language is so important to understand. When you can understand what is going on with someone's behavior, you can understand their feelings. When you understand their feelings, you can begin to find out the underlying thoughts that they have. This is about the closest thing to mind reading that you can ever truly attain.

To analyze other people, you have a simple process to get through—you must first find out the neutral baseline of behavior. This is the default behavior of the person. You must then begin to look for deviations in that neutral behavior. From there, you try to put together clusters of behaviors to find out what is going on in the mid of someone else, and then you analyze. This process is not difficult, and if you can learn how to do so, while also learning how to interpret the various types of body language, you will find that understanding other people could never be easier.

When to Analyze People Analyzing people is one of those skills that can be used in almost any context. You can use it at work, in personal relationships, in politics, religion, and even just in day-today life. Because of this versatility, you may find that you are constantly analyzing people, and that is okay. Remember, your unconscious mind already makes snapshot judgments about other people and their intentions, so you were already analyzing people, to begin with. Now, you are simply making an effort to ensure that those analyses are made in your conscious mind so you can be aware of them.

Now, let's take a look at several different compelling situations in which being able to analyze someone is a critical skill to know consciously:

In parenting: When you can analyze other people, you can begin to use those skills toward your children. Now, you may be thinking that a child's mind is not sophisticated enough to get a reliable read on, but remember, the child's feelings are usually entirely genuine. In essence, they have their feelings that they have, and though the reason behind those feelings may be less than compelling to you as a parent, that does not in any way dismiss the feelings. By being able to recognize the child's emotions, you can begin to understand what is going on in your child's mind, and that will allow you to parent calmly and more effectively.

In relationships: When you live with someone else, it can be incredibly easy to step on someone else's toes without realizing it. Of course, constantly stepping on the toes of someone else is likely to lead to some degree of resentment if it is never addressed. Yet, some people have a hard time discussing when they are uncomfortable or miserable. This is where being able to analyze someone else comes in—you will be able to tell what your partner's base emotions are when you interact, allowing you to play the role of support.

In the workplace: Especially if you interact with other people, you need to be able to analyze other people. You will be able to see how your coworkers view you, allowing you to change your behaviors to get the company image that you desire. Beyond just that, you may also work in a field that requires you to be able to get good reads on someone in the first place.

In public: When you are interacting with people in public, you need to be able to protect yourself. When you can read other people, you can find out whether you are safe or whether someone is threatening or suspicious. This means that you can prepare yourself no matter what the situation is to ensure that you are always ready to respond.

In an interview, you may find that read an interviewer's body language can give you a clue on when to change tactics or move on to something else. You will be able to tell how you are being taken simply by watching for body language and other nonverbal cues.

In other words, you deem the person speaking authority and therefore deem them to be trustworthy. Instead, make an effort to see the other party as what they truly are by learning to read their body language. You can tell if the politician on television is uncomfortable or lying simply by learning to analyze their behaviors.

In arguments: When you are arguing with someone else, usually, emotions are running high on both ends. No one is thinking clearly, and things that were not meant can be said. However, when you can analyze people, you can start to find out when someone else is getting emotional to disengage altogether.

In self-reflection: When you can analyze other people, you can start to analyze yourself as well. This means that you can stop and look at your body language to sort of check-in with yourself and find out what is going on in your mind.

Sometimes, it can be difficult to identify exactly how you are feeling, but this is the perfect way to do so in a pinch. If you can stop and self-reflect, you can identify your emotions.

In self-regulation: Identifying your emotions then lends itself to the ability to self-regulate. When you are, for example, in a heated argument and feel yourself tensing up and getting annoyed, you may be able to key into the fact that you are getting annoyed and respond accordingly. Conversely, when you can analyze other people, you can look at them and see how they are feeling. This means that if you can see that you are intimidating or making someone uncomfortable, you can make the necessary changes to your actions.

Chapter 27.How to use dark Psychology in your daily life

How Psychology Can Improve Your Life?

The following are some of the top ten realistic uses for psychology in regular life:

Get Prompted

Whether your purpose is to stop smoking, lose weight, or examine a new language, some training from psychology provides pointers for buying motivated. To grow your motivation while drawing close a project, make use of some of the subsequent tips derived from research in cognitive and educational psychology:

Introduce new or novel factors to hold your interest high.

Vary the series to help stave off boredom.

Study new matters that build on your present understanding.

Set clear goals that might be at once related to the assignment.

Enhance Your Management

Abilities It doesn't count number in case you're an office supervisor or a volunteer at a neighborhood teenage activity group, having true leadership abilities will in all likelihood, be vital sometime in the future for your existence. Now, not all of us is a born leader, but some easy suggestions taken from mental studies can help you improve your leadership capabilities.

One of the most famous research papers on this topic looked at three distinct management styles. Primarily based on the findings of this look at and subsequent studies, practice several the following when you are in a management function:

Offer clear steering but permit group contributors to voice opinions.

Communicate approximately possible answers to troubles with contributors to the group.

Focus on stimulating ideas and be inclined to praise creativity.

Come To Be A Better Communicator

Conversation involves a whole lot more than just the way you speak or write. Research indicates that nonverbal indicators make up a big portion of our interpersonal communications

Some key strategies encompass the subsequent:

Use proper eye contact.

Start noticing nonverbal indicators in others.

Learn to use your tone of voice to boost your message.

Learn To Better Understand

Others Just like nonverbal communication, your capacity to apprehend your emotions and the feelings of those around you perform an important role in your relationships and professional lifestyles. The time emotional intelligence refers to your potential to apprehend each of your emotions in addition to those of other human beings.

What can you do to emerge as more emotionally stable? Recall a few the subsequent techniques:

Cautiously assess your very own emotional reactions.

Record your enjoyment and emotions in a journal.

Try to see situations from the angle of a different person.

Make Extra Correct Selections

Studies in cognitive psychology supply a wealth of statistics about choice making. By making use of those techniques for your lifestyles, you can discover ways to make wiser choices. The following time you want to make a huge decision, strive the usage of several the subsequent techniques:

Try using the "Six Thinking Hats" technique with the aid of searching on the situation from multiple points of view, including rational, emotional, intuitive, creative, advantageous, and Dark views.

Recall the capacity prices and blessings of choice.

Appoint a grid evaluation approach that offers a score for how a selected decision will fulfill unique requirements you may have.

Enhance Your Reminiscence

Have you ever wondered why you can remember the precise information of childhood events yet forget the call of the new customer you met yesterday? Research on how we form new reminiscences as well as how and why we forget has caused some of the findings that can be implemented without delay in your daily life.

What are some methods you can grow your reminiscence of electricity?

Awareness of the data.

Rehearse what you have discovered.

Do away with distractions.

Make Wiser financial decisions

Nobel Prize-winning psychologist Daniel Kahneman and his colleague Amos Tversky performed a chain of research that looked at how humans manipulate uncertainty and danger while making decisions.

One looks at located that workers could extra than triple their financial savings by making use of some of the following strategies:

Don't procrastinate. Start investing savings now.

Commit earlier to dedicate quantities of your future profits in your retirement financial savings.

Try to be aware of non-public biases that may result in Dark money choices.

Get Higher Grades

The subsequent time you are tempted to whine about pop quizzes, midterms, or finals, consider that research has confirmed that taking checks honestly helps you better consider what you have learned, even if it wasn't on the test.

Every other study discovered that repeated check-taking might be a higher reminiscence aid than studying. College students who were tested again and again have been able to remember

61% of the content while the ones within the have a look at group recalled most effective 40%. How can you observe those findings to your lifestyles? While seeking to research new data, self-check frequently to cement what you have learnt, into your memory.

Become More Effective

Occasionally, it looks as if there are hundreds of books, blogs, and magazine articles telling us the way to get more completed in an afternoon. However, how much of this advice is based on real studies? As an example, think about the variety of times have you ever heard that multitasking can help you become more productive. Studies have discovered that trying to carry out multiple missions at the same time severely impairs pace, accuracy, and productiveness.

What classes from psychology can you operate to boom your productivity? Consider several the following:

Avoid multitasking while running on complex or dangerous obligations.

Cognizance at the venture at hand.

Eliminate distractions.

Be Healthier

Psychology also can be a useful device for improving your ordinary health. From approaches to encourage workout and better nutrients to new remedies for melancholy, the sector of fitness psychology gives a wealth of beneficial strategies that can help you to be more healthy and happier.

Some examples that you may practice at once in your very own existence:

Research has shown that both daylight and synthetic mild can reduce the symptoms of seasonal affective sickness.

Studies have demonstrated that exercise can contribute to more mental well-being.

Studies have determined that supporting people apprehend the dangers of bad behaviors can lead to healthier choices.

Chapter 28.Conclusion

I hope this book was informative and able to provide you with all of the tools you need to persuade people to do as you wish without them even being aware and to make the psychological choices appropriate for each unique situation.

The next step is to take all of the information you learned here and put it to use in any way you wish. Remember that to manipulate someone isn't always to take advantage of them. This power can do another a favor as much as it can be immoral. Regardless, how you choose to do so is up to only you. The eyes are said to be the windows to our soul and our thoughts. There is so much that you can tell just by looking at a person's eyes and the various movements that they make.

People often think that the easiest way to understand the human mind is by studying your own mind. Remember that you must analyze yourself first before others. It involves making a list of your own likes, dislikes, personality traits, values, needs, and requirements. Sometimes sitting down to do a complete analysis of we are complicated. However, it is an exercise that we must do at least once a month to know what we can improve and how to improve each day.

The daily activity of our life requires analysis, which allows us to perceive in retrospect the positive and negative consequences of our actions. One of the parameters used in the determination of who a person really is involves a study of their individual personalities. Personality defines a person and determines most of their actions and patterns of thought. Analyzing people through the determination of their personality is, therefore, one of the most accurate techniques that you can ever employ due to one simple reason. People cannot hide who they are for long.

Don't forget the knowledge of analyzing people, as it will ensure you'll achieve your goals. Remember the rules of persuasion, which is to remember to observe and appear trustworthy. Without reading body language and behavior, at least, you won't be as successful in persuasion with the rest of the knowledge you've gained. Finally, put all of these skills together to achieve the ultimate tactic of analyzing people. However you choose to use it.

DONALD BELFORT

Printed in Great Britain
by Amazon